Greatest Hits

By the same author

Tense Mood and Voice (Lyre-Bird Writers, Sydney, 1969)
The What of Sane (Prism Books, Sydney, 1971)
New Foundations (Poetry Society of Australia, Sydney, 1976)
A Nickel in My Mouth (Robin Hill Books, Flowerdale, 1979)
The Atlas (Black Lightning Press, Wentworth Falls, 1982)
Red Dirt (Paper Bark Press, Sydney, 1990)
The Streets Aren't for Dreamers (Shoestring Press, Nottingham, 1995)
Taking Queen Victoria to Inveresk (QVM&AG, Launceston, 1997)
Head and Shin (Walleah Press, Hobart, 2004)
Best Bitter (PressPress, Berry, 2006)
A Letter to Egon Kisch (Cornford Press, Launceston, 2007)
I Con (Salt, Cambridge, 2008)
Yeah No (PressPress, 2012)
The Unspeak Poems and other verses (Walleah Press, 2014)
Running Out of Entropy (Walleah Press, 2018)
Little Pataphysics (PressPress, 2021)

Greatest Hits: Poems 1968-2021

Tim Thorne

Selected by Lucie Thorne

PUNCHER & WATTMANN

© Lucienne Thorne

This book is copyright. Apart from any fair dealing for the purposes of study and research, criticism, review or as otherwise permitted under the Copyright Act, no part may be reproduced by any process without written permission. Inquiries should be made to the publisher.

First published in 2024
Published by Puncher & Wattmann
PO Box 279
Waratah NSW 2298

info@puncherandwattmann.com

NATIONAL
LIBRARY
OF AUSTRALIA

A catologue record for this book is available from The National Library of Australia.

ISBN   9781923099296

Cover Painting: detail from *(I Can't Get No) Patefaction*, by Lucie Thorne 2023
6 Salisbury Crescent drawing by Courtney Meacham 2019
Printed by Lightning Source International

Contents

Introduction by Lucie Thorne	11
Obituary by Tim Thorne	15
Emoh Ruo	19

from Head and Shin (2004)

Love Poem for Stephanie	20
Mother and Son	21
For My Father	22
… and a Pound of Round	24
The Aisles	25
The Living Are Left with Imagined Lives	27
At Table	28
Bronte Country	29
Leipzig	30
Black Cat and Wooden Shoe	31
Waldheim	32
Lockout	33
Lime Green Widgie	34
Writing with Viagra	36

from The Unspeak Poems and other verses (2014)

Love on a Brick	37
Are We There Yet?	38
Rainforest Triptych	41
Landing Card	43
Fall, Prince Edward Island	44
Principles	45
Clancy of the Cultural Studies Department	47
Advice to an Emerging Poet	48
Mother Superior and the Gardener	49
Scratched in Stone	50

From Margaret River to Homs   51
Piraeus   52
Revenge   53
Nature Poem   54
Anthrax Street, Lafayette TN   55
Fair and Balanced   56

from Running Out of Entropy (2018)
Land and Language   57
Fukushima Suite   72
    Motherhood   72
    Don't Touch the Air   73
    Kawamata Silk   74
    Shadowland School   75
    Miyakoji, All Clear   76
    Plume-Gate   77
    Spring Thaw, Daiichi   78

    from Lieber/Stoller:
Kansas City   79
Big Mama   80
Spanish Harlem   81
A Hot Bowl of Soup and a Shave   82
Is That All There Is?   83
    from Home Invasion:
Theft   84
Dispossession   85
    from Lank Tree:
Blackbird of Peace   86
Buddha and Wind Farm, South Australia   87
May Day   88
Chile, September 1973   89
Anzac Bargain   90
Summer Poem   91

The Antipodean Adventures of DJ Donny Johnny   93

from Taking Queen Victoria to Inveresk (1997)
Fruit and Flowers   125
Sunday in the Gardens   127
Naming the Sensation #2   128

from New Foundations (1976)
Autumn   130
    I. Behind the Phoenix Foundry   130
    II. Fisherman   131
    III. Against Mallarmé   131

from Five Trees;
    Acacia Melanoxylon   133
    Casuarina Stricta   134
    Myoporum Insulare   135
December, Palo Alto   136
Somewhere Between Waxahatchie and Woonsocket   137

from A Nickel in My Mouth (1979)
The Worst Journey In the World   141
80° 08' 1934   143
Onyx River   144
Gardening is the Opiate of the Elite   145
Vanzetti   148
Waiting for Franco to Die   149

from Tense Mood and Voice (1969)
    Star   150
Proem   150
Sequence   151
Crystal Palace   152
Pain   153

Envoi   154

from The What of Sane *(1971)*
Whatever Happened to Conway Twitty?   156
High Country   157
Sideflower   159
Man and Law   160

from The Atlas *(1982)*
II   162
III   165
V   167
Interlude (By the Greystone bed..   170
XVI   171

from Red Dirt *(1990)*
   from Red Dirt I
Low Tide, North Esk   172
Macquarie House   173
Brady's Lookout   174
Reds   176
Songs of the Protest Era   178
   from White Diamond Gloom
Fluid   179
Blade   180
   from Red Dirt II
Grammar   181
Song for Seychelles   182

from The Streets Aren't for Dreamers *(1995)*
Stage Dive   184
Words for K   186
Arramaieda at the Oak   187
Arriving in Devonport   188

Bear	189

from Thorne's Best Bitter (2006)

Mesopotamian Suite	190
1. Ace	190
2. Fallujah Face-off, April 2004	191
3. Two Purty Gals from West Virginia	192
4. Shake 'n' Bake	193
5. The Code of Hammurabi	194
6. Bagdad Bazaar	194
7. Alabama	195
8. Purrfect Angelz	196
9. And the Poets Fled	197
Dentist's Waiting Room	198
Villanelles of the New Morality	199

from A Letter to Egon Kisch (2007)

VIII	202
XII	202

from Yeah No (2012)

La Cave d'Aristide	210
Write the Future	212
Gnomic	213
Gallarta	214
Suburban Subversion	215
Elegy for Shelton	216

Little Pataphysics (2021)

Little Patronage	217
Little Patchwork	218
Little Patagonia	218
Little Patch	219

Little Patriach	219
Little Patefaction	220
Little Patchouli	220
Little Paterson	221
Little Patible	221
Little Patella	222
Little Patisserie	222
Little Patrician	223
Little Patrick White	223
Little Patriotism	224
Little Patricide	224
Little Patmos	225

previously Unpublished

The Golden Mile	226
Chemo	227
Epitaph	228
Notes	229

Introduction

In September 2021 I got the call that Dad had been taken into palliative care and didn't have long to live. I was living on a mate's organic farm in Lindendale in Northern NSW at the time, having accidentally relocated there in early 2020, with the pandemic having blown out any semblance of my previous reality as a full-time touring musician. As the state borders were still closed, a bureaucratic hoopla ensued - but a week later I was fortunate enough to be granted special consideration to fly to Tasmania, under the proviso that I would spend 14 days in isolated quarantine. So with Tim in hospital, our darling Mama Stephanie moved in with my big sister Clare for the fortnight, and I spent those 14 days in self-isolation at Mum & Dad's, in the house I grew up in, 6 Salisbury Crescent, West Launceston.

Tim died four days later. Those next ten days were long strange days… in physical isolation, surrounded by our lifetimes of memories. I started obsessively listening through Tim & Stephie's alphabetised LP collection, working my way backward from Warren Zevon. I started preparing what I would say at Tim's Wake - trying to prepare a speech *to* and *for* Stephanie… all about their Grand and Radical Love Story, and trying to find the words to describe my amazing Dad. A man who possessed a truly brilliant mind, a profoundly generous spirit and a mighty heart. So smart, so funny, and sometimes such a know-it-all pain in the arse.

To our immense shock, Stephanie died just a few weeks after Tim.

In the months that followed, and tasked with sorting through that big old house, I read every book of Tim's poems from cover to cover. I trawled the folders of manuscripts and unpublished works, the scraps and the miscellany, the reams of writings. Immersing myself in his extraordinary output and brimming with questions I'd never get to ask.

In Tim's study — filed neatly on the top shelf of the cupboard that held all the most important papers —I found Tim's self-penned Obituary (classic Tim!) which follows this introduction. There too, directly below the obituary, was 'Epitaph', the final poem in this selection, and likely the last poem he wrote.

Tim & Stephanie lived at 6 Salisbury Crescent for over fifty years. It was a home filled with love, art, music, conversation, laughter, ideas and community. Poetry and poets. The beautiful drawing of their house reproduced here was made by our wonderful friend Courtney Meacham on the occasion of Tim & Stephanie's 50th Wedding Anniversary in 2019. So many of these poems were written at Tim's desk — looking out from his study window, behind that towering eucalyptus.

Today would have been Tim's 80th birthday. It seems a fitting day to try and write a short introduction to such a prodigious body of work, Tim Thorne's *Greatest Hits* — gathered together and sent out into the world, with love, from your troubadaughter,

Lucienne
25.03.24

6 Salisbury Crescent, West Launceston

Obituary

Tim Thorne 25/3/1944 —

Please feel free to add to, subtract from or otherwise alter the following. If you prefer, substitute material about an entirely different person.

David Rennie was born on March 25th, 1944, at the St Ives private hospital in Launceston to Betty Kent Hughes and John Rennie, who had married a few days earlier. Betty was a nurse and had to live in nurses' quarters, so there was no way David could live with her. He was adopted by Alan and Nita Thorne, a couple of school teachers with no children of their own, and renamed Timothy Colin.

As a child Tim lived in various places around Tasmania as his father was the 'Headmaster' (as the terminology was then) of schools at Sprent, Yolla, Glenorchy and Burnie. His secondary education, which he didn't particularly enjoy, was at Burnie High School. Incidents he often recounted from his high school days were: being kicked out of the boys' choir at the request of the other boys because he couldn't sing a note; playing 'chicken' by standing in teachers' car park spots; wagging classes to play pool, only to run into the Deputy Headmaster coming out of the bookmaker's downstairs from the pool hall; being removed by the Headmaster from the ballot paper for election of school prefects, and various other acts of minor rebellion. What he did get from his formal education, however, and retained throughout his life, was a love of poetry.

At University he learned more about the craft of poetry, joined the Literary Society, campaigned for justice for sacked professor Sydney Orr, made some lifelong friends and joined the Old Nick Company, writing scripts for the Uni Revue, Infradig.

It was during this show that he met Stephanie, realising very soon that she was the person he wanted to spend his life with. Their first date was a shopping expedition to buy a pair of high-heeled shoes ... for Tim.

After a brief stint teaching at Ulverstone, Tim went to Sydney, where he established his career as a poet, returning to Tasmania in 1969 to teach at Kings Meadows High School. 1969 was a highlight year in Tim's life; in July his first book was published, in August he married Stephanie and in September Richmond won the premiership.

In 1971 he and Stephanie left to spend a year in California, as Tim had been the recipient of the Stanford Writing Scholarship. Soon after they returned they bought the house in Salisbury Crescent which became home for over 50 years.

This was the time of the war against Vietnam and of military conscription in Australia. Tim took part in many aspects of the campaigns against these and thought hard about the kind of society that had led to them. This led him to a deep and fervent belief in Marxist socialism, which he maintained all his life. During the 1970s he was twice elected as a delegate to the ALP's National Conference, and played a leading role in organisations such as the Unemployed Workers' Union and the Northern Youth Shelter. He was also an active member of the Tasmanian Teachers' Federation, the Modern Language Teachers' Association and the Launceston Film Society. Never convinced that party political programs alone could solve society's problems, he saw the ALP as a useful platform in the short term and let his membership lapse after a few years.

The quality of Tim's poetry was recognised by the Australia Council, who granted him a series of fellowships, enabling him to resign from teaching and write full-time. As he could do this from home, and as Stephanie wanted to continue her career, he became a "househusband", something rare in those days and still not common enough. By this time, Clare and Lucie had been born, bringing great joy to his life, as they continued to do right up until its end.

In 1985 Tim founded the Tasmanian Poetry Festival, which he ran for 17 years. In 1988 he took on the job of Community Arts Officer for the Tamar region, a job which he held until the funding ran out in 1993. While working in this capacity he met many wonderfully creative people, including some with different sets of abilities. After the job finished he remained interested in fostering the artistic abilities of people who had been marginalised. He was an active member of DADAA (Disability and the Arts, Disadvantage and the Arts Australia), serving as National Secretary for a couple of years.

Many people, readers of the Hobart Mercury at the time, would remember Tim as a witty and iconoclastic columnist for that newspaper, a role he filled from 1986 until 2003. Back in the 1970s he had been the Australian's poetry reviewer, and over several years he wrote reviews for the Sunday Tasmanian. For a variety of reasons, all these positions were terminated. He used to boast that he had been sacked from three different Murdoch newspapers.

Being aware of how Tasmanian poets found it difficult to get published, Tim set up Cornford Press, which he ran for about 15 years, providing an outlet not just for locals but also mainland writers. This was hardly a profitable venture, but Tim never put making money ahead of making opportunities for those who needed them. As well, Tim wrote 16 published collections of his own poetry and won several major awards. He also conducted poetry workshops in a great variety of community institutions, from prisons to museums and trade unions. One of the written works of which he was proudest was the text he created for the memorial at Inveresk to Tasmanian workers who had been killed at work.

In 1996 Tim made contact with his birth mother and discovered a whole new set of family connections. His biological father had already died by the time Tim tried to find him, but

Tim was able to establish contact with his half brothers, Mike and Paul Rennie, and to meet their families. He visited Betty regularly at her home in Bendigo and was grateful to have three years of the maternal love she had been prevented from displaying for all those decades.

By the early years of this millennium, Tim's two granddaughters, Zoe and Ruby, had been born, bringing even more delight to his and Stephanie's lives. As he shed his work commitments, sliding gradually into retirement, he found more time for two of his passions, political activity and gardening. The garden at Salisbury Crescent flourished. Tim became active in TAP (originally Tasmanians Against the PulpMill, later TAP into a better Tasmania), serving as its President for a few years, and in the SEARCH (Social Education, Action & Research Concerning Humanity) Foundation, spending six years on its Committee, including one year as Vice-President and one as President. The principles on which the SEARCH Foundation is based are the principles he held dear all his life: democracy, socialism, environmental sustainability and opposition to all forms of discrimination. It is as an upholder of these values, as well as a loving family man, a one-eyed Richmond supporter and a talented poet, that he would like to be remembered. It probably won't be as a singer.

Emoh Ruo

My poems are cladding,
washable, weatherproof.
What is inside is not
just a home; it's a house.

A white tyre is a swan
is a metaphor. En-
jambements roll, wagon wheels.
Stanzas are garden beds.

Structure and patterning
need tough material:
vinyl and pebble-dash,
birdseye maple veneer.

Reader, wipe your feet on
my jokey welcome mat.
Come in. Get comfortable.
Mi casa su casa.

It's more than a building,
more than a collection;
it's an investment in
iconic literature.

from *Head and Shin* (2004)

Love Poem for Stephanie

When we talk it should be
in Cocoliche or Baracoon,
some creole we can live in,
built from the tentative pidgin
of cultures touching lightly
like trade, like skin, learning
each other, working past
getting and giving to love.

When we move there should be
strange names for what we do
towards each other. No dance,
gambit or skater's leap
is new enough to make
such unnatural demands
on the lexicon of contact
and release, trust and surprise.

Mother and Son

It's March again, our month. Now
it's a different hospital, a different city.
We talk above the nebuliser's roar:
part chainsaw, part surf, all edge.

The spasms of pain are at closer intervals
as you labor, this time to postpone
the separation. Your skin's cross-stitched
with butterflies and bruises.

Your hands, which I never heard play Poulenc,
never fast enough, you said,
grip, but mine keep slipping
as I slipped away from you those years ago.

Holding on isn't always everything. Skin slides.
Too tough to die, too proud to call this living,
you hug into these punctuated hours
our missed half-century of love.

For My Father

My friends are writing elegies for their fathers.
I have so much to say about you, and memories
have nothing to do with it. We never met.
You have conned me even more effectively
than all your other gulls and marks.
You conned me into being. Forty years
I held you dead hero or at least Kilroy.

Then when you really died I became
your ghost. Your hairline, chin and gait
returned to haunt those who barely mourned,
while you still con me and I fall for it
again, giving you life.

                        No doubt you wore
the Flying Officer's uniform more dashingly
the night you conned my mother than I wear
your face and limbs. Nothing I have written
has had a punchline half as sharp
as Grandmother's signature when you put it
on your prize fiction work, her will.

Did you ever imagine my fantasies,
and was that why you had all those medals
no-one ever won who never left
Sale or Laverton except on leave or awol?
We picked the same *Boys' Own* stories
to not grow out of.

                    Once I wrote,
"Seeking heroics, we become absurd."
But that was about me. You found heroics
easy as any pose: judge, doctor, engineer.

Post-modern before your time, you had
more style than Walter Mitty. Once you shaped up
against an angry neighbour who had inches,
stone and skill on you. He backed away.

I've swapped audacity for irony.
You never pretended to be
anything less than excellent.
No wonder you could not acknowledge me.

... and a Pound of Round

Taking the festival posters around,
went into the butcher's shop in the Quadrant.
The old guy came up to the counter.

"Poetry eh?
Had a bloke in the shop the other day
talking about poetry
I told him: 'Shakespeare,
Shakespeare's the best poet there ever was.'
He said to me, 'What about Wordsworth, eh?'
'Wordsworth? He was English wasn't he?'
The one I always like is that feller
Mansfield. You know:
'I must go down to the seas again.'
That one comes to me mind
every time I go down to the beach
at night like. Yeah
I do a bit of fishin'.
'The lonely sea and the sky.'
Yeah. That'd be my favourite.
Course you can put a poster on the door."

The Aisles

In Greece, he'd sing some sort of hymn like this t'ye:
                    —Byron, *Don Juan, Canto III*

The poets and postcards were right.
The Aegean is as blue as Toilet Duck,
but I wouldn't drink wine that shade of dark.

On Hydra, "le Johnston de nos jours",
I soak up my own light aura of pretension
along with the retsina splashed by sun

and play at being the poet playing at
being the tourist. This is by way of
a snapshot getting from the isles

where burning Byron ... and you know the rest,
including the history of the one island
which consistently sold out,

to the Venetians, the Turks and now the Yanks.
And Karamanlis died today,
le Menzies de leurs jours.

So I drink at the Sun Set Bar
halfway between Disco Heaven
and the yacht club's bikinis

and watch the wakes, like chips of temple marble,
slice neat as Visa cards across the path
of Pheobus plunging with his dazzling trolley.

"Yet in these times he might have done much worse:"
George's irony was less cliff than balcony.

The view's still clear, the octopus delicious.

Liberation's not a phallic ruin,
a flag-stripe against the sky,
a flush of azure on the porcelain.

The world's shelves are wiped
clean as sunlight. They are stocked
with meditations on antiquity.

The Living Are Left with Imagined Lives

i.m. Robert Harris

You will not add age's load to wisdom's.
It would have been superfluous, anyway,
best left for those who need a longer lease.
You carried, you said, the sins of the city
on your shoulders, no bed or desk so awkward
that the lies it had produced could not be straightened
round the narrowest stair-turnings of the heart.

So much that hasn't died sings darkly:
Piaf's hollow bones as flutes for fire,
each albatross rigging the clouds with wit,
scraps of sad Jane whenever light meets stone,
but, mostly, tough love as the skin on old words
yet still too slippery for the nets
the honest eclipse has dropped between us.

"A million golden birds of future vigour"
you wished me once. What skies of mine they've graced
have been the more open for the memory
of your discourse, its hard innocence,
of courage lacking calculation,
your blunt face butting at the truth.

At Table

i.m. Gwen Harwood

Aperitifs and antipasto
bring talk of weather, friends and work.
The consommé's as rich as music.
Arias of conversation
slip, *glissando*, round the room.

Miss Foster's no longer in the office.
Perched no longer on her desk,
she's flying through these soft exchanges.
As the table's cleared for entrée
the topic turns to literature.

Mutability *in situ*:
red replaces chardonnay
Russell, Wittgenstein and Ayer,
epistemology and how
to live; the main course is consumed.

Yet change implies something's remembered.
Light as a playful sorbet, words
are strong, not just to cleanse and sweeten.
Time is a tongue that's hinged and mobile.
The softest palate's backed by bone.

Layer after layer's vanished.
No-one's at the table now.
Night's as black as bitter coffee.
Miss Foster's no longer in the office.
They never could keep track of her.

Bronte Country

I swear I saw Branwell, young again,
in a pub in Haworth through the karaoke crowd.
I remembered Doris Leadbetter's story of the village drunk
who sat in the corner "an' Branwell were the village drunk before me,
an' this were 'is chair." This dark-curled American tourist, all Pre-Raphaelite
and solitary with his bitter, not playing the pokies and definitely not
looking at the historical prints of railway scenes as monochrome as the skyline,
TV antennae and all, on a day no brighter than the parsonage,
sat, still as the couch on which Emily died but better preserved,
his eyes the colour of the tumbling gravestones up on the hill
or the shadows that hide, waiting for the sunlight
when they will skid like fictitious siblings,
a source of visible delight
but unnecessary.

Leipzig

Against Honecker's hoons
the *Gewandhaus* was sanctuary.
Masur stopped the show,
was a safe conductor.
Music, after all, formed
with Party and Sport
the Trinity.

Now *Deutschland über Alles*
in the square drowns out Bach
and Irving's apologia for Adolf
proves freedom of speech.
Where is the sanctuary
for those who shot through
the wall to the dole queues?

A 14-year-old girl with
shoulders as big as all of Prussia
does lonely laps in water
clean of chemicals and blood
against the clock,
against the clock.

Black Cat and Wooden Shoe

Joe Hill "wouldn't be found dead in the state of Utah"
so his ashes went to Wobblies round the world.
Australia's portion was seized in a raid
before it could be decently interred
in the Botanical Gardens, ended up
in the fireplace of Central Police Station, Sydney,
not keeping the coppers nearly hot enough
so they warmed up by running through the streets
scraping off walls Tom Barker's poster,
the one urging bosses, parsons, editors
and landlords to war and workers to follow them.

It got hotter still when Tom was jailed.
Simpson's Bond Store, Stedman's, Winn's
all burned as beacons of war-bond investment,
Bryant and May the opposition spokesmen
for liberty. Better fire than blood,
or let the politicians cut their own throats
to dowse the flaming struggle.

Waldheim

Purged from the Ulverstone Club lest it be seen
as fostering "a continent of Germans
and mongrels, or of yellow races",
Gustav trekked up to Cradle
six months after sweet Kate's death
to their forest home, their hideaway,
with memories of peace and tenderness.

The stove he lugged in was "heavy machinery",
the clothes line "a wireless aerial".
Why else would an enemy alien
want to command the high ground
except to spy, to sabotage, to cook up ways
of killing the nephews of the gentlemen
of the Ulverstone Club over in Flanders?

The Siegfried Line stretched to Daisy Dell, Dove Lake,
to keep the currawongs and ring-tails in Prussian discipline
and make the mountain ash grow Junker-straight?
While farmhands died twisted in Somme mud
the cockies here were all up-front for Hughes
and Empire Loyalty, but thankful for the secret ballot
to vote against conscripting the next crops's harvesters.

So Gustav stayed on the mountain, knew
the wildflowers' true subversion and the snow,
yelled in whatever Austrian dialect he needed
around the summits, into the storms.
His hermit's sanity under gross hewn beams
was a star way above the cultivated valleys
until the world could climb to meet him.

Lockout

Next-door were lucky; they had cookery books,
read recipes around the table when they were hungry.
We didn't even have that. It was scab or starve.
John Brown had said, "Let them eat grass."
We held out. Dad was solid. Mum was a bunch of twigs.

Most of them were returned men, too, the ones
that were fired on at Rothbury, but some were kids,
or older, too slow or too naive to be safe,
like the old bloke who looked like he was tied
to the roadside gravel by a skein of blood

from his stomach, trying to push himself up,
or the young feller with two bullets lodged
in the loose skin under his jaw. But he survived,
which is more than our Norm did
after the dum-dum got him in the guts.

Cessnock lost 25 cricket teams thanks to
the lockout. Men who'd come through
Gallipoli, Salonika, the Dublin Post Office
or jail as COs only to be shot by Aussies found
if they won't let you work, you can't afford to play.

You know a town is really desperate
when the evangelists come to scavenge.
They filled one of the pits with water,
turned it into a great baptismal bath
to save whole families for John Brown's Jesus.

Lime Green Widgie

Twelve or thirteen,
used to go foxin'.
I was the youngest:
kept cockatoo.
Down Fern Glade or
up by the waterfall,
never caught anyone
— somethin' to do.
I was always stalkin'
my lime-green widgie,
singin' Buddy Holly songs
and wearin' Mitchell blue.

Friday night shopping
up and down Wilson Street,
never bought anythin'
just hangin' roun'.
Wish I looked like Elvis.
Wish I played the guitar.
Wanna do somethin'
to shake this town.
My lime-green widgie,
teased hair and tight skirt,
cardigan buttoned up
wrong way round.

Sittin' in the Bluebird,
milkshakes and jukebox,
standin' roun' the doorway
at the surf club dance,
wore all the right clothes,
denim and pink socks.
Never had a Harley.

Never had a chance.

My lime-green widgie
worked at the pulp mill,
dated blokes with genuine
grease on their pants.

So there went yesterday
wobblin' on her high heels
into tomorrow,
leavin' me blue
and I'm still stalkin'
my lime-green widgie,
singin' Jimmy Clanton songs.
And I'm 62.

Writing with Viagra

She said she hoped I wouldn't be offended, but ...
I said, "Nothing ever offends me",
forgetting for the moment
war, poverty, racism, sexism, child abuse and the Liberal Party
—as you do—
"I've got a present for you", she said
and gave me a pen,
white, with a blue clip on which was stamped "Pfizer"
and strong red Vs like ticks all over it.
I use it to write soft, tender, limpid love poems.
Once I loaned it to another poet
and she snapped the clip off.
It had got loose and wobbly anyway.

I wasn't offended.

from *The Unspeak Poems and other verses* (2014)

Love on a Brick

"Love" impressed on a convict brick
instead of an arrow shows that someone soared
out of Van Diemens Land's cold mud.
The word still soars out of its baked clay prison.
Which way did it face? Were rats and possums
the only witnesses? Or did it bless
a family from a warm hearth, not only
as reminder, reproach or simple wish,
but with its heritage of defiance,
with its own vector, surer than any bolt?

Of all the slogans despair could write,
of all the cries for justice or revenge,
this was the word chosen. Of all the ways
that love could be sent, through air, flesh, paper,
to choose clay was a masterstroke.
A message baked into a house
has lived beyond memory just as clay
was and will be what we are.

Love strong enough to stamp bricks
can smash chains, file through bars,
disarm screws, trick dogs and fly.
Through what weather? It has not landed yet.
Even in these ruins it has kept hale
and pure, its object always clearer
than authority, more compelling.
We shall build cities with such bricks.

Are We There Yet?

When I grow up I want to be Corey Worthington
because not only can I use the word "insouciance" correctly,
but I can pronounce it with just enough of a French accent
to indicate that it almost belongs in Narre Warren.
But mostly it's because of the yellow plastic sunnies
and the parties. When I grow up
I want to almost belong in Narre Warren.
I want to be an early adopter
of alcopops, tatts and 'tude.
When told to take a good, hard look at myself,
I want to be able to respond:
"I have, and so have millions. And they liked what they saw."

More role model than mentor,
Corey is leading me along the path
on which I followed my parents years ago:
from red bricks and roses out to the new,
from a certitude that nestled
between Schadenfreude Gardens and Sigmund Freud Park,
past the comfort of the last railway station
to the raw limitless edge
where symmetry imposed on the void
partly hides the basalt and brown grass,
and smooth kerbs channel excess fluids and fears.
Rock blunts scissors. Paper wraps questions.
Assertion cuts deep.

Fillmore Pops was a mentor.
Half-Cherokee, half-Negro
was how he described himself in '72.
Fillmore Pops taught me how to drink Thunderbird
undetected in the back seat of a Greyhound.
You've got to get down below the level

of the seat in front, make sure the driver
can't see the brown paper bag. No-one drinks
soft drink from a bottle in a paper bag.
Getting down that far's not easy, 'cause that's where
the stowaways hide. DeWane
was down there on the ride when I met Fillmore Pops:
Sacramento to LA. Eighteen and lookin'
for a job, a hustle, who knows? On the run
from…? Who would ask? We shared
the Thunderbird with DeWane.
Fillmore Pops also shared his thoughts
on eating. Avoid the bus station food;
buy the makings and live on salami-cheese-tomato sandwiches.

I have seen more grown men cry
on a Greyhound than on any other form of transport.
Take the Friday night bus out of El Paso or Miami
and you don't need the TV news from any disaster zone.
I have seen empty bottles floating on the tears
that flood the floors of those buses. I have heard
men pleading with the driver to let them off
on a freeway in the middle of the Everglades or the desert,
death being preferable to the desolation
of sitting any longer in that community of travelling souls
where the lights of every town you pass through
hit you like a verse of a Hank Williams song.
Trains, on the other hand, are for hope.
Paper wraps rock. Scissors cut valentines.
Love blunts perception.

When I was a kid we used to play
chicken with trains, teachers' cars, each other,
but never with tanks.
That little bloke in Beijing '89
with his shopping bags and his nifty footwork

set a level to aspire to, beyond
the usual guns and batons. He was a hero
of Hanna-Barbera proportions.
It was the bags that clinched it. What was in them?

If I fill my own calico bags
with ethical contents, can I then
as I shuffle my ill-rehearsed sidesteps
claim some place? Empty stubbies,
torn-up betting slips, butts, used condoms:
the swag we carry as we dance against
what crushes. How capacious are the saddlebags
as we switch genres, mosey along
down by the ol' Rio Tinto?

Answer the big questions.
It's art if it covers that patch of mould
on the spare room wall. It's truth
if that skinny chick in the Oxfam shop
read it somewhere. It's life if
you can laugh at it, like synchronised goldfish.
For most of the others a simple "no"
is enough. Scissors cut paper.
Rock blunts hope. Poetry wraps nothing.

Rainforest Triptych

1. Heartwood

The black at the heart of the sassafras,
prized by those who respect what they destroy,
(as the best hangmen or woodworkers do)
is an infection. The best selling heartwood
has green and white torsades that writhe and whorl
through the black. The bacterium
that makes the letter opener or paperweight
such a pretty souvenir needs the living tree.

So does the Macleay's swallowtail;
its black, green, white dance alive
around and through the sassafras.
Respect is sometimes cheap as a galliard.

Where the heartwood's butterfly colours lie
the gallery is clean as stainless steel.
The corpse has been carved with clarity
and ticketed. The germs survive.

2. Trunk

The bootsole skids down across the fallen trunk,
negating nature. Khaki, yellow, grey combined
to make the moss's singular green, now slashed
where the whole spectrum's been absorbed.
What changes? Temperature, angle,
most of all the way the bark interacts
with what it feeds as it decays.

Here, where cloud can seem more solid than rocks
and water can grow faster than insects,
here the very concept of paradox
is turned on its head. Two thousand generations
have known the rainforest both commands
and enables respect. Here what lives
because of the bark is a soft chain of life.

3. The Iconography of Protest

Dolerite is not easy to love. Dermasol
does not lend itself either
to eros or charity. Rain storms
that shatter the air only obscure
the picturesque. There has never been
a Wilderness Society can rattler
dressed as a cumulonimbus
or a lerp. What is easy
is to confuse the aesthetic
with the political.

The Dombrovskis photo of Rock Island Bend
turned nature into a weapon
for self-defence. Of course art changes
the world, but what matters more than a poster
on a stylish wall is the dialectic
of blood and water, stone and wind.

Landing Card

On the landing card at "Reason for Visit"
I've ticked "Business".
The immigration officer, too young
to be my daughter, asks,
"What's your business?"
I answer, "Poetry."
I've also ticked that I'm bringing
into the country "commercial goods".
I answer her next question, "Books."
"Will you be selling any books?"
Ah, will I? I set the playlist
of possible answers to "Shuffle"
and say, "I certainly hope so."

My smile, back there at "Poetry",
was intended as "diffident", "engaging",
almost "self-deprecating", possibly
"collusive", as in, "You and I both know
that poetry's not really a 'business'."
Her reaction was so blank
that it registered as less even
than the flicker of a thought I'd had
when filling out the form
that a poetry book is not just a
"commercial good", but a good
unqualified.

Fall, Prince Edward Island

for Libby Oughton

The maple leaves are pinned to the sidewalks
by their black spots. The cruise ship,
unpinned to anything but deep
oceans of money, sails out.
The soup kitchen is closed for Thanksgiving.
(Let them eat turkey.)
But the beach is still red: not Anne's hair red,
but as flagrant. Sand should be paler,
demure, to be walked on.
A family celebrates holiday
warm against what will arrive.
Love trails bare toes through the transgressive sand.

Principles

My father stayed out of gaol all his life,
or so I hear. Family pride.
Back as many generations as I can check,
and forward a couple: same story.
Police holding cells don't count.

Snarling at an empty cop car
doesn't do you much good, but then
what does? "Cheats never prosper,"
was a childhood chant. That was back
in the days before we understood
about real estate, politics and poetry.
Nobody ever got rich as a direct result
of obeying the law. Democracy's
when the bastards win. Any other system
means they don't even have to compete.

One morning a beggar in William Street
held out his hand to me. In it was more
money than I owned. Admittedly
it was payday. By that afternoon
he'd gone. Feeling rich again, I thought
his job has more risks than mine. Life's not about
fairness. (My job was legit as I recall.)

Kath Fallon had a character who said
she'd rather be hit than smiled at.
Didn't know how to fight a smile.
Wordsworth said the world's with us too much.
Racine said, "No money, no Swiss", but Mest said
to throw cheese at the government.
Redgum said that if you don't fight you lose.
I say if you don't fight you don't win.

If you do fight you lose.
Keep fighting.

Clancy of the Cultural Studies Department

I had written him a letter. Now, I know that there are better
ways of making contact but I did have his address.
I had looked him up on Google but the pickings there were frugal
and he hasn't got a mobile so I couldn't SMS.

Then an answer came by email from a post-grad student (female).
Shook me up so much I nearly dropped my laptop in the spa
and when I managed to retrieve it I just could not believe it.
"Clancy's been deconstructed and we don't know where he are."

In my academic fancy non-visions come of Clancy
no longer prowling libraries or the student union bar.
Vanished thanks to Derrida: not even dead and buried a
worse fate could not have been his had he been hit by a car.

Now, I'll say this about Clancy; there's not the slightest chance he
has risen up to Heaven where good theoreticians go,
where with sempiternal patience they lie round swapping dissertations
on French films, fashion, Fantales, football, fisting and Foucault.

It quite gives me the vapours as I sit here marking papers
to think that Clancy disappeared with so much still to learn.
I can't imagine his life ended, so I'll call it an extended
sabbatical from which he is unlikely to return.

Just as sure as Sid killed Nancy, there's no way I'd change with Clancy,
Having lost corporeality I know I wouldn't cope,
while he spent his days at writing and faculty infighting
and his nights at bonking students and smoking lots of dope.

Advice to an Emerging Poet

Know nothing. Write as if you know. Offend,
the more the better. Beauty's anodyne;
avoid it. Readers will misapprehend
wildly, but remember Wittgenstein
has all the answers, so you should pretend
depth, while on the surface every line
seems only to present mundane despairs.
This will not win you prizes, but who cares?

Doctors have their Hippocratic Oath.
The language is your patient, so be sure
you do no harm. You should therefore be loath
to operate unless it will secure
your satisfaction and the rapid growth
of self-esteem. No benchmark is as pure.
Critics and cops are there to make life hard.
Plead guilty and they sometimes drop their guard.

Mother Superior and the Gardener

In the Carmelite convent the Mother Superior
thought a lawn in the quadrangle would be the go
so the nuns had a change from the bleaker and drearier
greys of the walls as they walked to and fro.
She engaged a celebrity gardener, in theory a
respectable man with his own TV show.

Now the vast frozen wastes of furthest Siberia
were no more remote from the world than this place.
Any godfearing nun would succumb to hysteria
if she knew what ideas some people embrace.
The gardener was red as a monkey's posterior;
of Christian beliefs he had not the least trace.

He had two kinds of grass seed and let them both trickle
in a pattern. The lawn came up, true to his hope:
dark green on light green grass, hammer and sickle,
beneath which could be read the words: "Fuck the Pope."

Scratched in Stone

On the wall of a cell in Richmond Castle:
"The only war worth fighting is the class war."
1916: A few men brave enough to be called cowards
knew there would be no war
if no-one obeyed. The first step
led to a stone wall. What was scratched on that wall
is there still. Refusal
is the only weapon they can't take from you.
When a kid in the firing squad
(They always picked the youngest.)
chose not to shoot, he was next.

Now, as then, the only enemy
is whoever says, "You have an enemy."
Whether they bark it from between
a waxed moustache and a row of gongs
or squeeze it like pus onto a Murdoch column,
the message will dissolve or morph.
New alliances, trade links: the world
flows and rolls like money.
What is scratched into the stone of a cell wall
is what you read, clear and strong,
as the door slams like a rifle volley.

From Margaret River to Homs

Between the vineyards, on both sides
of the roads that run to the beaches,
the arum lilies, feral through the scrub,
make the place look like one
of the less imaginative funeral parlours
of my childhood, the ones that specialised
in clean death. Meanwhile
in Baba Amr death is no less clean
despite the rubble. What's left of life
is jagged with fear, matted, twisted beyond
breath, wearing the desire for freedom
like dreadlocks. Tears divide the dust
on kids' faces. There are no lilies here,
no wine. No surf roars in like shellfire.

Piraeus

i.m. Alexandros Grigoropoulos

The city's only skyscraper
still flips the world the bird
but its twenty-storey billboard
no longer holds Johnnie Walker
or Cristiano Ronaldo mid-stride.
At its foot the Filoxenia Taverna
has closed down. My "Please explain"
gets the expected answer.

As Aeschylus knew, the exit
is stage left. This tragedy
was written inside another skyscraper
in Frankfurt where the archaeologists
come from. And where the pensions go.
I used to drink Heineken here
without irony, enjoying a bar
that proclaimed love of foreigners.

The blokes who'd scrambled here
somehow, from Africa, offered more
than pirated CDs or sunnies.
A smiled *"Ochi"* and a slight wave away
were enough in the sun
and the diesel smell of work.
No hard feelings. But no tax exemptions
for ship owners. Austerity (from the Greek.)

Revenge

After the stingray got stuck into Steve
someone had the bright idea to leave
dozens of killed rays stranded on the beaches:
"eye for an eye", a bright idea that reaches
back to the old bloodthirsty bits of the Bible,
when everything was primitive and tribal.

When Top End crocs make lunch of German tourists
the rifles come out. "Sentimental purists"
is what we conservationists get called.
Like Sunnis and Shiites, peace talks all have stalled.
Now Brocky's gone will someone tell me please:
do we wipe out more Holdens or cut down more trees?

Nature Poem

"...redesigning the natural world...and embarking on an Orwellian future..."
— *Prince Charles on genetically modified food*

"Orwellian?" That's a good one, Chas.
As in *Newspeak*, as in using language
to mislead, as in choosing to say
"redesigning', which tells us
there was an original designer.
So biotechnologically "enhanced"
food is ungodly, as distinct
from GE-free communion wafers
which, being of the natural world,
contain its living maker, who then
can go on making it and its bread
inside digesting humans who are neither
inside nature nor out, just next to it?
Does that explain why nature is made up
of genes? Darwin, Escher, Stelarc,
are you all on board or waving off
our embarkation from the airport bar?

Are the Monsanto whitecoats somewhere plotting
to redesign the supernatural world?
If so, can we put it down
to human nature?

Anthrax Street, Lafayette TN

"People stand back when they read the name
of the street on my checks," she said.
"They should change it to America Street
or Freedom Street. They think I'm a terrorist."

Which makes her, I guess, a terrorist suspect
and therefore permanently guilty
of having been a suspect, despite her smart clothes,
her hair as blond as anthrax.

To protect the immune system of the social body,
close the post offices, the schools, the courts.
Prescribe a sixty day course of Cipro
or bomb Afghanistan? Prevention beats cure.

One street might be just spore-sized
against the victim spread to shining sea,
its mass awaiting destruction,
cutaneous or inhaled, but we all know…

They should rebadge. America spores,
freedom spores (and there'll be fries with that)
will reassure when we pay by cheque
that the nation has a healthy balance.

Fair and Balanced

(Fox News slogan)

"It is unpatriotic to report civilian casualties."

We have suffered thousands of civilian casualties.
We now have an annual Civilian Casualty Day.
There is a civilian casualty industry: shrines, flowers,
in memoriam verse to order. Civilian casualties
are almost firemen in their beatitude.
Heroic civilian casualties brought down Flight 93,
their cell phones exploding with patriotism.

"No, it's unpatriotic to report *their* civilian casualties."

The Afghan who was over six feet tall
and so might have been Osama,
the exuberant wedding guests, the families
dining at Saddam's favourite restaurant,
the raped kid burned to kill the evidence,
grannies in one-way crossfire, the passengers
in what they claimed were ambulances:

they shall amount to zero, otherwise
our reporting appears neutral and neutrality
is inappropriate when one side is the other side.

from *Running Out of Entropy* (2018)

Land and Language

Begins through cot bars, is where
cold is. Not self, not blanket.
All vowels and volume the first plaint:
the initial landscape misted, inchoate.
... *et lux erat* but it was a while coming.
And when it did, there was the territory.

Floorboards, doorways, sunlight
but always something to be read as mother.
The rubber smell of the bottle's teat
cut into the warm. The real mother's
absence, which might well be
back projection, recorded as pyloric reflex,
projectile spew marking locus.

Love knits all. A one-eyed teddy bear
in a saved snap grins below what memory can mine.
Others had the phrases for what
was lived, images curiously lodged
in today's brain. Lifted up on VJ Day
to the sky: "You're too little to know
what it's all about." Even the fake kiss
on Times Square that day had more authenticity.

In suburban Launceston in a back yard
a warm, full nappy was merely comfort.
There was no pop psych to explain
offering, product, pride. It was a matter
of waiting until words could be accepted
and the judges were old school (literally:

that single storey brick one a few blocks away)
hence the recalled utterance, "dingobardy"
pure dada, phatic joke, family legend.

Always counterpointing infancy's
sweet chaos were the mechanics
of getting places: hard work, a small car,
a country posting. Dad sweated and swotted
evenings towards a BA, taking the bumps
of philosophy with no teammates in the valley
except on the footy ground. Words, paragraphs
came and went by slow post over the hilly roads,
a van of language jostling the spuds and the milk.

My mouth was too slow to imitate
the turkeys in the next paddock.
My gob-ble gob-ble made me realise
that human speech was less than universal,
nor would I be fattened for Christmas.
There was a gap wider than the fence
with its three strands strained at soft grey posts,
singing in gales, perch for other birds,
between what my voice could do:
demanding, chortling, asking why,
and how the feathered dinners
over there made themselves heard.

And words could be seen, glimpsed from
the schoolrooms where my parents taught,
a room each, the whole school, while I played outside,
too young to join the kids who'd been corralled
down from the forest clearings, the trappers' huts,
the sawmills and scratched out farm blocks.

Leaking through the windows of that school's two rooms
into the corridor where the tricycle's confined laps palled
and the bright wooden blocks had exhausted
all permutations of architectural fantasy,
the link between sounds and those lines,
straight and curved, the shapes, closed and open,
filling the blackboard with intricate stripes,
became clear: education by osmosis! Until, miraculous,
as years of family retelling have confirmed,
I read aloud the Vegemite label. *Us-e in sand*

Beneath the school's stilts the swamp
bred tigers and copperheads, mossies, frogs,
a whole cycle of eat-die-feed where we humans
were disadvantaged except for the thrilling
patterns that sang our social skill
there, on that board, and in the air we owned.

The old languages were never mentioned.
Only a few generations before,
the *palawa kani* would have bounced off trees
or been breathed soft as campfire smoke.
Speech is not what pours from slit throats.

The King's English in lines of rhyming verse
bound the classroom globe with red ribbons
and there we were, some kind of afterthought,
sliding off the bottom like the drop of blood
when I cut my toe with the axe, trying
to chop wood the way the big boys did.

The King, whose profile on the pennies
spoke reassuringly of calm,
of peace after the hell of Changi
and the worse hells we hadn't heard of then,

was a stutterer, like Danny down the road,
but Danny never had a film made,
never got lessons from Geoffrey Rush.
Danny milked the cows and chopped the wood
without cutting his toe. The stutter never stopped
Danny being king of the valley.

Next door was the oval, where play had rules,
scores were kept, the goalposts never moved.
The university, not so bound by tradition
despite its sandstone, shifted what it wanted to shift,
made two years' study pointless. Dad took up golf.

****

Mark used to hang around the links.
Near the dog-leg third was a boggy patch
where you could always find balls to sell.
One day he'd park his own flash car
by the clubhouse. One day he'd be able
to read the signage, the rules, even the menus.

****

Sally had always sat in the front row,
smiling at knowledge, gulping concepts
like milk at recess and laughing out
her own fantasies, thoughts, as words
grew and interacted, as synapses clicked
smoothly as the cycles of the farm
she would escape from. The low gleam
of the butter factory vats
was never going to be enough
to light her travelling.

When she moved to the city, to Uni,
her days were full of ideas juicy as nectarines,
heavy as late picked figs. Weekends and nights
she waited on tables. Penalty rates
bought text books. Tips went to the maitre d'.

****

When the sky to the west is heavy with bruises
then light with the quick clarity of flashed gold,
count the seconds till the thunder comes.
Weather, like the economy,
doesn't need an epithet. "In for some weather..."
In for some austerity. At least the floods
and bushfires come from our own mountains.
Yet we know even that's not true.
There are no borders in the atmosphere.
Carbon seeks asylum where it can.
Meanwhile the sawmill's been bought out, closed down.
Over a long lunch with harbour view
somewhere between the *Vosne-Romanée*
and the *Arturo Fuente*, "Our people will
talk to yours," and not even a handshake's needed.

In that two-room school one of the lessons
was, "hard work brings rewards." What was never said
was to whom. Nor was it taught
how a signature, like a lightning bolt, can turn
generations of skill and knowledge
to ash. Omission is a lie.

****

When the McCafferty's bus from Melbourne
pulled in behind the BP servo

I first met my mother, apart, that is,
from the passing acquaintance which had been my birth.

I still feel the pressure of her hand
As she held mine all day, greedy
for the lost loving. We talked of music:
Satie, Poulenc, her granddaughter's songs.

Mostly, we babbled. What poured out
were all the betrayals, her father
and mine, the web of siblings, generations of women
"bossy, forthright and intelligent" as if it were a motto.

What can be claimed? The family territory
fills maps whose colours bleed to torn margins,
whose legends list alchemical signs.
What's decorative? What's real?

False binaries are no help.
Nature/nurture debates roll in tides,
leaving the present an uncertain plane,
but you wouldn't have it otherwise,
would you? Family is not just where you live,
it's what you build there, what you can't see
yet absorb. It is like language.
It is a language, but more complex than most.

As for my father, the one I never knew,
the one who didn't play any team sport,
not even education, what of him?

There is no language without lies.
There is no land that cannot be left.
He flew his Spitfire into glory.

Propelled by the fuel of words he ranged
through all the loftier professions,
judge, doctor, engineer, in the war

disciplined for "wearing an officer's uniform
to which he was not entitled"
("That's how he conned me, the bastard," my mother said.)

If things had been different... but they couldn't have;
he and the practical world made sure of that.
What words would I have eaten, bled, explored?

How would I have been in my place?
The other end of the same suburb, it turned out
for a while, the tamed creeks, the smell

of bread and pubs, mown grass and cars,
pastel houses herded by factories,
his end the zinc works, ours the tannery.

Here the schools were brick again, tumultuous,
with musset huts as well, to catch the speech bubbles
that floated like European gas above where kids

baked or froze in their metal, where phrases, accents
bounced off the asphalt playgrounds
like bald tennis balls, skinned knees

or childish crushes. Poetry
snuck in somehow, maybe through
the tiny slit in the steel nib that was meant

for sums and copperplate, spilling
with the other blotches, smudges and mistakes
onto the paper with its unforgiving lines.

****

Words woo. The strings and strains
of grammar's rituals deserve
an Attenborough's reverent commentary.
See how the male constructs his phrase.
Watch while the woman reads and smiles.

Lies aside, there's always slipperiness;
distortion is the verso of desire.
Download whichever love song tickles
your fancy, Schubert or Barry White.
"Come live with me and..." read my book.

Venus in Blue Jeans, Lancelot:
romance is a sub-category
of fiction. Without the lust, without
Mr Darcy rising from the lake
as Excalibur, how would any sentence read?

The muse is long discredited
as an excuse for inspired work,
but still we write to mate and so
we lose a little of ourselves
with every phoneme, and of the world.

****

Even the wedge-tail knows to stop growing.
The tick on the possum swells until
it drops engorged. Grasses run to seed
but no further. Millennia of compressed life
under what some call "overburden"
(language shaping the world again),
others the rock that sustains and flavours wine,

can rest there, the earth as haven.
Metaphysicians and economists
dabble in what can't be seen, although
it can be felt, can twist and crush.
The finite is marvel enough.

****

The kindling Danny used to chop was from bush
long replaced by ranks of *nitens*. Danny sold
the farm when the supermarkets put the squeeze
on the milk company. The house and sheds
meant the land was worth less. "Encumbered,"
they reckoned. What his grandfather had built
with love and blisters, craft and myrtle, strength,
was an encumbrance. They took most of a day
to demolish and burn the lot. That was time lost
from planting tree-weeds, laying baits, dodging tax.

Danny doesn't stutter when he's drunk.
Now he spends more time not stuttering.
He flows through the streets of the town,
smoother than he looks. Piss stains and stubble
are thin between him and pain. Buy him a drink
and he'll pour you a pint of words. He'll tell you
stories his grandmother told
from the old country, the country where
the land still provides after centuries
of crops and tales and soft rain.

****

Mark carted logs. It was safer than felling
and with three kids, well, you need to be safe.
From the coupe to the chipper, one-fifty k:

two hours on the road if you did it legal,
but most days you could squeeze an extra trip,
'cause one trip's worth more than a speeding fine.
Couple more years and the rig'd've been paid off,
then they said they couldn't sell the chips.
The bank took the rig back. The company went bust.
The bank took the mill back. Mark had a bit of super.
The bank went bust. Most of the super went.
There's a new yacht off Nice. Its skipper says
he got sick of boardrooms.

****

Sally fell in love. Her life,
gregarious as facebook, was a lit
path to marriage, children, everything bright
as the valley autumns she remembered.
He was a bit controlling. She liked that in a man.
He drank, but didn't everybody? The first time
he hit her he cried with remorse.
It got harder to cover the bruises

with make-up or excuses. The kids, too...
Sally's leaving the refuge soon
but the paper AVOs are written on
gets soggy in spring drizzle.

****

Language travels on a wet road,
can spin without warning.
Polysyllabic words were always dodgy
but it's the pronouns that are most dangerous,
"we" the worst of all, unless it is
so full of meaning that it's open, empty.

Until we are not who we are but how,
when we are not merely everyone
nor even everything, but patterns.
not links but chains, beyond taxonomy,

language crashes and maims, sideswipes
truth as if it were a wallaby. Discourse
or roadkill: there is still a choice.
"Defence", "progress", "renewable" must have earned
their drivers enough demerit points by now
that they'll be garaged in perpetuity.
Nor let us forget that "illegal immigrants"
are neither, "flexibility" constrains
and "drought" is a short-term cop-out word.

****

The valley's dirt, sweet with rain and light,
was a long time building forest.
The forest killed, now the elements
make only trees. The old cliché
about not seeing the wood holds true.

Flash quolls and flasher parrots can't compete
with smiling eyes twinkling like atrazine
from healthy faces, Sweden to Sarawak,
well fed, well financed, smooth as a *nitens* leaf.
Empson's line reverberates:

The waste remains. The waste remains and kills.
Books on endangered species, ballot papers
that might get counted, toilet rolls,
these are how civilisation measures
victory over the sweet intricacies.

****

My T-shirt was made in Bangladesh.
It doesn't burn me or crush my shoulders,
nothing as simple as that, and while I wear it
I can't see the label but when I do I know,
consumer or citizen, we pay to kill.

Fair trade coffee washes down
the free range eggs. Join the picket line
outside the co-op. You can sign
The online petition without being able
to write your own name any better
than your average Ok Tedi mine worker.
Click and your heart sings along
with Simon and Garfunkel or Billy Bragg
even if you're not quite sure of the lyrics.
Cycle, recycle, check, recheck
how ethically comfy your super is.

****

Who owns Danny's farm land now? Who owns
Mark's truck? In Zurich, Macau, Manhattan,
there is fine merino cloth crafted to drape
suavity and confidence. Does one choose
the tie to match the single malt, or drink
something complementary to the silk?

Small matter. As the permafrost
roars its methane countdown all the clocks
are in accord and their percussion
welcomes Gehenna. Who owns those
who own the owners? There is a point
at which the questions disappear.

****

But what does not, will not disappear
is the energy of what is owned.
The boundary fence's wire is taut,
the better to delineate,
but the birds that sing on it have shapes
out of picture books, the grasses throb
with green on both its sides.

                    I went back
after sixty years and saw that the old school
was square on its stilts. A tiger snake
shimmied ahead of me through the tall twitch
beside the football ground. There are not enough
men in the valley now to make a team.
The scoreboard stands like a narrow victory,
the goalposts no doubt firewood years ago
thanks to an axe like Danny's and a need
like all of ours for focal heat,
but someone still mows the oval:
municipal order, civic dopamine.

****

We shall stand, an encumbrance, in the way,
Danny and I, singing without a stutter,
Sally doing gleeful harmonies.
And Mark's three kids will stand with us and sing
and the song will be of the forests, but the song
will be of the singing. Our song
will be heard in Arrernte and Euskara;
it will be heard as if it were in tune
or sweet cacophony. It will be heard.

Music is a barricade they can't dismantle.
Victor Jara sang unaccompanied
after they chopped his fingers off.
His lyrics, Lorca's, all those heady chants
while linked arms made human chords:
Abramos todas las jaulas
Let's open all the cages
and delight in the notes that escape.

We can sing back the valley,
the dead factories, even the golf course,
but only with a network of noise.
I see the football field with no goalposts,
no competing teams; everyone wins
in all the valleys, all the suburbs
where the chords have been crafted.

But first the realisation
that no friesian ever milked herself,
nor is it possible for capital
to surrender. Land is clever
but not magical. Language
does not exist until it's made.

And then resolve: from the last forests,
from the escarpment mists
and from the beaches where tidal promises
or threats impend, resolve to make
lyrics for everybody's hit parades.

We have what's needed. History is a shed,
DNA a toolbox. The human brain
was wired for compassion long before
it built a web of contradictions.

We have material. In fact we have
nothing else. Any two bits of it
rubbed together will be enough.

Fiat lux ... What is important is
listening to the soil and to each other.

Then, united, whole, diverse, create.

Fukushima Suite

Motherhood

Fukushima, the mother of all
nuclear meltdowns, has gifted
radiant oysters to Vancouver Island.
The amniotic ocean in slow spin
delivers change, brings Hello Kitty catfish;
hentai squid with beguiling big eyes
appeal to the maternal in all of us,
even the least pacific of dudded
islanders drowning already in salt.

Yes, we're all up against the wall, mother,
far (could you believe?) from the promises
we always doubted anyway.

Sometimes I feel like an adopted child.

The misshapen pearls would burn your ears.
The sliding flesh no longer nourishes
but *Madre de Dios!* The nacre
swirls inside the shell, luminous.

Don't Touch the Air

Yes, you can play outside, but...
Meanwhile ten thousand ks away
Missouri snowflakes click the counter,
and here the experts have all reached
their permissible levels. Fixing
the problem is now a job for those
who have no idea. We have no idea.
There is an idea, somewhere, in memories
of Little Boy. This little boy, three,
looks out the window to where
he has never been, to where
the problem is invisible and patient.

Beneath him they are building a wall of ice
to keep the sickness in the earth.
Once it came from the air, then from the sea.
There is no nurturing element, only
a mother's warning love, fierce
as fire, strong as atoms.

Kawamata Silk

Kawamata silk from Fukushima
is the finest in the world. It takes
eighteen strands to equal the thickness
of a human hair. The effects of radiation
on gall-forming aphids are well documented.
Yet to be seen are the results
of similar studies on Kawamata silkworms.

The traditional aesthetic is such
that Hokusai's "Great Wave" could not be imagined
breaking over cherry blossom:
everything in its proper orbit.
2011's great wave broke outside the borders
of the woodblock just before the viewing season.
The traditional aesthetic melted down.

The cherry blossom of Fukushima,
as buoyant as silk, is still viewed
for traditional aesthetic reasons.
It has not been inspected for deformities.
The thinnest tissue is spun
to cover everything delicately
but as firmly as tradition.

Shadowland School

Weeds cover the playground
at Iitoi Elementary. No-one comes to oil the swing.
No-one comes to push it.
From Tokyo they send advice.

Old people stay because they need
not just any home and because
the contamination line was drawn
down the hill, closer to the plant.

The wind can't read. The school principal
has received a poster showing
happy children dusting themselves down
before coming indoors.

She looks at these pictures.
She waits. The line does not move
but the wind plays like a running child
not wearing a mask.

The old people of Iitoi
can't read but they don't need words
from across a line drawn by someone
with a map in an office.

Miyakoji, All Clear

After three years of the rising tide
living in boxes in the car park
we have been given the all-clear.
We still measure our lives in millisieverts
but now Grandfather no longer needs
to be a Klansman in Tyvek
going back for an hour or two a year
to dust the Buddha, lament
the veggie garden and gather
overexposed wedding photos.

We have been given to understand
that down at Daiichi
the leaks in the decontamination system
will soon be fixed.

We have been given to understand
that the cores
will only plunge as far as bedrock
and stay there inert.

Plume-Gate

"You have no idea what's coming. It's going to send us back to the Stone Age."
— Trailer for the movie Godzilla

Conspiracy theories seep like isotopes.
When was that photo taken? When did you ever
trust the corporation? In the more ornate
corners of the Internet fear explodes
with all the certainty of metal. Cybersteam
signals let the globe know what
distrust dictates.

          Sci-fi has inured us
so that the fissures between reason
and complacency have become
the space around a nucleus, a home
to withstand bombardment, room to play
safely with predictions. The not knowing
Is energy, drives rumours, fuels
resistance.

          Meanwhile from the Yakuza
to Mossad to the ATF, wherever
blame can blaze or fiction can insert
its truth, there will be narratives.
Indignation, half-quotes, misspellings,
racist tangents make a slurry
that cannot be disturbed lest the monster wake.

Spring Thaw, Daiichi

The caesium drifted down with each unique flake
as the cold cracked the concrete
and the thaw poured through.

The tanks shift only slightly. Everything
settles somewhere, sometime, even
families, memories, possessions.

Where are the snows of yesteryear?
The poet's question sticks in the brain
like strontium 90 in the bones.

This year's snows next year will be
in the supermarket, in the blood,
pouring from Spring to Spring.

from *Lieber/Stoller*

Kansas City

Neither Jerry nor Mike had been to Kansas City
when they wrote about a bottle of its wine,
Teenage erotic fantasies are rarely
so geographically perverse.
While Missouri's adolescent boys
dreamed of California beaches
where every grain of sand is a starlet's shy nipple
Jerry and Mike were after that KC Lovin',

which was the original title when
Little Willie Littlefield recorded
what we know as "Kansas City"
where they had "a crazy way of lovin'."
Twelfth and Vine intersected
like neural pathways at some musical G-spot
where the rhythm and blues are orgasmic
"and I'm gonna get me some."

Big Mama

That was when Jerry found out he was white,
when Willie Mae said, "Don't you be tellin' me
how to sing the blues." One look
at the razor scars on her face and he almost didn't
sing "Hound Dog" himself the way he'd written it
for her, but when she got it and put 300 pounds
of guts and gravel, howls and sex
into it, the world was remade.

She'd been around: gospel to joints,
Alabama honey to bourbon and chicks
in LA, call and response. It took this song
for her to hit '52 with the gender subversion
it barely understood, to be heard
telling the man to quit snoopin' round
her sexuality, her pride and her voice.
Jerry was 19, should have been easy pickings.

Spanish Harlem

A rose is a rose is a fist. In Spanish Harlem
something grows up between the *marqueta*
and the New York People's Church,
but it is not thornless like Ben E. King's voice;
Cha Cha Jimenez of the Young Lords
should have sung it. Mike only wrote the intro;
it was Phil Spector who teamed with Jerry on this one,
but even he didn't let it rip flesh.

There is a rose and there is the scent
of death that grows up in the street,
"right up through the concrete" where the struggle
is too urgent for "soft and sweet
and dreaming." When even the moon is on the run
how will we fight back?
Hard decisions can hide in a soft melody
and in lyrics that have never seen the sun.

They indicted Cha Cha eighteen times
in six weeks. They killed Julio Roldàn,
José Lind and Manuel Ramos. Here and in Chicago
there was more blood than the rose needed.
Despite Aretha changing the words,
shifting locale and race, the Rainbow Coalition
held out and now the Nuyorican rappers
flourish in Jerry's, in everybody's garden.

A Hot Bowl of Soup and a Shave

When the Monkees came to Sydney and waved
anti-war banners from the balcony
of their suite at the Sheraton
to the demo outside, Bob Gould
stuck up a sapling with only his oratory
and commitment saving him
from ridicule, D. W. Washburn was flying
from the gutter to the top of the charts,

hobo chic before Waits or Bukowski.
Jerry and Mike knew a jaunty tune
would do more than charity could,
would convince us that doin' fine
with a bottle of wine was all the rhyme
that was needed, that being vertical
on a corner in Kansas City, LA or Kings Cross
was literally a step up in the world.

Meanwhile the war was telling us
that a hot bowl of soup and a shave
were not enough to get anyone out
of the gutters where poison and blood
flowed together and even a group
as concocted as the Monkees could hear
the screams of Viet kids and know
what was down and what was out.

Is That All There Is?

Gaby had known Thomas Mann's "Disillusionment".
Niece of Edmund Husserl, she'd fled the Nazis,
found refuge with Jerry. Now Peggy Lee
was asking the nihilists' question
straight from the late nineteenth century.
Nietzsche had written God's obit
long before this LA smartass turned it into pop
channeled through Gaby's beauty and fear.

Peggy was blonde enough to ask the question
anywhere even though she sang jazz.
She could have been carried out of a burning house
in her pyjamas without attracting
persecution. Jerry was lucky but he knew.
The booze and the ball were almost all
about escape, but not quite.
Phenomenology in a pop song?

Well, if the circus can't impress a child
what hope for lived embodiment? What hope
for love, for justice? From Uncle Edmund
Gaby Rodgers *née* Rosenberg
had learned *Enttäuschung*, had earned
her cynicism in Europe. Hollywood
was way out of its league and the question
remains. Is that all there is?

from *Home Invasion*

Theft

The maps that teased my childhood were silent.
The imagination they cosseted
was of no use. Instead of song
there was a flatness, a sheet of pastel shades.
I could find Peru, but not food.

And these maps were my inheritance.
Maps can be owned. Land is something else.
Maps can be stolen. When the atlas claps shut
those who are trapped between its pages
have no co-ordinates of place.

"Grab and go" is the usual way:
jewellery, cash, phones, then out and off.
It is different when what you take remains.
Too big to move and where would you put it?
And yet what can this be called but theft?

There were no trinkets to steal, no devices.
This was not mere burglary. What was taken
and sold came from the deep and mineral heart
of the place, of the premises.
It was a crime even to call it property.

Maps that are sung, that sing
in and through memory, that are not maps
but the land itself, that dance and are danced:
when these are gone the world has disappeared
and all its denizens are hollowed out.

Dispossession

for Ronnie Summers

Country music grew in the cities.
Lives shredded by the need to work,
to find work, sing of the honky tonk of loss.
This side of the ocean the fringed shirt
covers a displaced heart like a minor chord.

Borrowed music never heals. At best
it cleans wounds. So does alcohol.
The songs that flow through country like blood
can still pump knowledge, read tracks, string shells
despite the fusillade of bugles, drums and fear.

These only leave flesh wounds. The marching bands
of empire could only for a while
drown out the ancient concert of the land.
Pop tunes hit the top of the charts with a bullet
that ricochets off the bone.

Meanwhile a long way from Nashville
lost cowboys strike chords that let pain
trickle through simple melodies
and a Stetson shades more than can be heard
of breakage, dislocation and of hope.

from *Lank Tree*

"*We have been plucked from the world of commonsense,
Fondling between our hands some shining loot,
Wife, mother, beach, fisticuffs, eloquence,
As the lank tree cherishes every distorted shoot.*"
— Francis Webb, "Ward Two"

The Blackbird of Peace

Is peace anywhere other than on the wish list
of every beauty pageant contestant?
While we check out the beheading meme
the cat sits waiting for the pie to hatch
Four'n Twenty hours of the news channel
ignore the politics and the taste.
The market and the market place

reveal the dialectic of desert war. Ignore
the chant, the nursery rhyme, the steam
that escapes with the birds on the corporate logo,
where only 18 of them are free of the pastry
and able to fly as sweetly as any beauty queen
straight as a volley of Exocets. The other six,
held in eternal takeoff, also began to sing,
are still beginning to sing.
The sauce is on the pie. The pie is in the face.
The drone is above the village.
The king is in his counting house.

Buddha and Wind Farm, South Australia

Over Cactus Canyon (Who do these people
think they are? Lost cowboys shooting it out
on the Escarpment just a Colt's shot from the vines?
Hardy abseilers of some dry peyote cliffs?)
the world's most aggressive Buddha (All it needs
is a ten-gallon stetson and some aesthetically tooled
leather, and it would be at home, or at least
as close to home as the nearest gunfight.) stands ready.

Here on the Fleurieu (rhymes with cheerio) Peninsula
listening to Jimmy Dowling's "English Lesson"
and so thinking of languages and learning
I remember Mary Beckwith, the convict who "accompanied"
Baudin back to Europe in his bed. We sell
words, wine, religion, bodies. By the banks
of the Yattagolonga I lay down and wept
for all the canyons that will be cactus.

But the wind turbines sang to me of hope
and of the triumph of beauty over faith.
Their blessings flowed like pure grenache
or energy from blades white as logic.
Mary's entry into recorded history, too,
was logical. When exploitation
is a given, strike the best bargain,
be quick on the draw and shoot straight.

May Day

The banners flow down the street
like the blood at Peterloo or Marikana.
Some red dries to brown. Some lives
scarlet, pumps through the heart
of humanity as fast as a fire engine
and as loud. Each year we link
more than arms across the stream,
across the decades. Joe Hill
never died, said he. George Loveless
came back from Van Diemens Land
in a secular resurrection.
The uniforms vary. The need is constant
for each of us to become all of us.

Chile, September 1973

When Salvador chested the rifle
held by some callow corporal
who barely knew who he was,
who barely knew why,
who barely knew anything but orders,
he had love and justice
to counter the bullet,
but love and justice were too big, too widely given,
too easily pierced by one narrow shot.

Victor, when your songs had to be killed,
They chopped your fingers off.
They didn't know that your guitar
loved liberty enough to play itself
while you sang until they chopped off
everything else of you, including
twenty thousand of your audience.

They lied about those last seconds in the Moneda,
claiming Salvador had killed himself.
They lied about you, saying you had sung
your songs unaccompanied at the end.
We know better. We know that your guitar
held more humanity than all Kissinger's thugs,
and that, around the world, it still
accompanies a growing choir of voices.

Anzac Bargain

A pre-recorded minute of silence will cost only $2.20.
Or you can download it for free,
and wouldn't that be the sort of thing they died for?
The right to get away with stuff? The larrikin tradition?

At that rate you could get the Cage piece for about ten bucks.
That's if you were into highbrow silence.
Mind you, that's $1056
for a good night's sleep.

No matter how much you offer I won't shut up
about how they shouldn't have been there,
about how disobedience is the best weapon
and how the officers on both sides are always the enemy.

Summer Poem

Lying in the semi-shade
with Kent MacCarter's *Sputnik's Cousin* spread open
across my chest, my hat balanced
on nose and forehead,
from time to time I pluck the cords
that hold the hammock,
Ray Brown without the heritage of slavery:
all "Work Song" and no work.

The typeface is too small for the dappled light
the *E viminalis* allows. After misreading
"kaftan" instead of "Kafkan" on the back cover
and being distracted by memories of Adrian Rawlins
at some festival when the weather was just like this,
I closed my eyes and listened to the waterfall
and the birds, whom we falsely accuse of singing
even though the sounds they make have different origins.

Poets, too, face similar charges,
equally without substance, except in cases
like Lauren Williams or Bob Dylan.
I muse for a while on the word "bard"
but (blame it on the warmth) I get distracted again,
remembering a sign, part of *Sculpture by the Sea*
a few years back: "Don't feed the bards."
Distraction is a seasonal luxury.

Meanwhile Kent MacCarter's poems lie unread
and constructing a clearly articulated and sustained
poetic argument is something that will have to wait
until Autumn sees the hammock put away,
or even longer. Ray Brown died after playing golf.
What kind of a word is "Kafkan", anyway?

What's wrong with "Kafkaesque", which was good enough for the writers I read before I acquired a hammock.

The Antipodean Adventures of DJ Donny Johnny

Dear reader, you'll recall we left our hero
Desiring sudden and complete retirement
From the scene or else we'd rate at zero
His chances of survival. This desire meant
Flying somewhere. Rio de Janeiro?
Hong Kong? New York? Of course his chief requirement
Was uneventful and sequestered rest.
Seychelles, they say, is quite by far the best

Of all the world's remoter beauty spots
To hide away in when the mind needs calming.
Luxury resorts and fancy yachts
Abound and the inhabitants are charming,
The visitors sometimes less so, for lots
Of dubious types turn up there. It's alarming
To contemplate how wealthy Eurotrash
Can ruin paradise by flashing cash.

Donny, while loitering, languid, on the terrace
Of the Pirates' Arms, a watering hole
Frequented by beachcomber and by heiress
Alike, got talking with a friendly soul,
American it seemed but, reader, whereas
Some from that nation tend to think the whole
World is their playground, I've met quite a few
Who're decent fellows, as, I'm sure, have you.

Randy was the name of this young Yank.
He owned a yacht, a yawl to be precise,
The *Biped Mermaid* was her name, quite swank
In her appointments. She'd already twice

Sailed round the world, he mentioned as they drank,
Surviving everything from Arctic ice
To tropic cyclones and lots more beside.
She could take any weather in her stride.

"In fact, my friend," said Randy, "I'd regale ya
With many a tale if I but had the time
About how not the slightest hint of failure
Has ever marked her journeys. She's sublime!
We're just about to sail her to Australia.
We're taking on provisions here then I'm
Off as soon as I've found a first mate.
The one I had has flown back to Kuwait.

"Some family business there. He had to sell
Or buy (I'm not too certain) for his wives
Something or other, maybe an oil well.
Or minor sheikhdom. Just like that, he hives
Off, leaves us stranded, what the hell!
Some folk can really stuff up others' lives.
I don't suppose…" Donny said, "I can sail.
My uncle had a yawl, the *Profane Grail.*"

An ocean voyage could be just the thing,
Our hero thought. They strolled to the marina.
There lay the *Biped Mermaid.* Neighbouring
Craft, though handsome, all looked somewhat meaner
Next to her. Randy said, "Wait. I'll bring
The crew to meet you. " Now DJ had seen her
He loved all forty foot of her, from mizzen
To jib. His wanderlust had really risen.

He checked her out: mahogany and oak,
With dacron sails, bronze fittings, stainless steel
Rigging, she was what most seafaring folk

Would love to sail on. Down to her very keel
She'd won him. Randy seemed a decent bloke,
So when he came back they soon sealed a deal.
"OK, we sail tomorrow then," said Randy,
"Now meet your shipmates, Mandi, Candi, Brandi."

Donny felt as if he'd found himself
Inside *Good As Gold* by Joseph Heller,
A novel that should be on every shelf.
Seek it at your second-hand bookseller.
But I digress. I must remind myself
That this is not lit. crit., that I'm the teller
Of a tale, to which I must with haste return.
It's of our Donny's story you would learn.

These three attractive women, young, curvaceous,
Looked up in unison and smiled in greeting.
DJ Donny's smile and nod were gracious
As he shook each proffered hand, repeating
Each name and managing to keep salacious
Thoughts well hidden though his heart was beating
A fraction faster than its normal rhythm
At the thought of sharing one small cabin with 'em.

Duly provisioned, early the next day
The *Biped Mermaid* set out, heading east
Past spinner dolphins frolicking at play.
The tropic sun shone down without the least
Cloudlet and very soon La Digue, Mahé
And the whole archipelago had ceased
To be in sight. No tiniest misgiving
Troubled Donny, who just thought, "This is living."

That afternoon, sunning themselves on deck,
Wearing only lotion, Candi, Brandi

And Mandi asked Donny if he'd kindly check
The contents of a duffle bag that Randy
Had stowed under a transom. "Just a sec,"
Said Donny, very pleased to be a handy
Servant to these beauties. He retrieved it
And what he found inside—who'd have believed it?

A little plastic sachet of cocaine.
From within the cockpit Randy's voice
Called out, "I guess that out here on the main
It's not against the law. We have the choice
Whether to indulge or not. It's plain
That you three girls are dying to rejoice
In a little snort. How about you?"
This last to Don, who said, "I'd like some, too."

They carded up ten lines, two for each nose
(One for each nostril, you could also say.)
Randy said to the girls, "I don't suppose
You'd have a fifty-dollar bill." There was no way
Between their pretty heads and pretty toes
A pocket could be found. He said, "OK,
I'll use a hundred." Then he rolled a note
And sniffed his two lines, every single mote.

Dear reader, it is not my role to preach,
Or to pontificate on wrong and right.
I merely tell what happened. Surely each
Of you may (be your morals lax or tight)
Pass judgement, but please, please, I do beseech
You, not on me, no matter how you might
Wish to shoot the messenger. Just as it
Is I tell it, hostage to moral hazard.

And so, without regard to long-term danger,
Dissolving septa, psychosis or worse,
The three partook, then Don, himself no stranger
To the magic snow, far from averse
To any substance likely to derange a
Part of his senses, sniffed his share. The curse
Of the moneyed classes has been the description
Of coke by those who uphold its proscription.

But, as I said, enough of moralising.
The five of them proceeded to have fun.
The powder was, at first, quite energising.
They danced, made out, then as the setting sun
Blazed gold and crimson, turning the horizon
Into a sheet of flame as quickly done
As started (Ah, those tropic sundowns!) dropped
To their bunks and soon all movement stopped.

But not for long. Donny felt a hand
Upon his shoulder as he lay in bed.
Mandi it was. "I know you'll understand,"
She whispered, "But when everybody's dead
Asleep a girl gets lonely." As her tanned
Breasts swung gently just above his head
Pity on her plight caused him, though yawning,
To offer company until the morning.

They snuggled close together. What transpired
Between them, reader, I'll leave you to guess.
Not much imagination is required,
I'm sure. Then Mandi's cry, "Yes, Donny! Yes!"
Must have been louder than she'd have desired.
Although it wasn't uttered in distress,
It caused young Candi, in the other bunk,
To wake and wonder loudly, "Have we sunk?"

It wasn't long before she ascertained
The reason for the noise. She slipped across
The space between the berths. Now the cocaine'd
Worn off, her mood was black and with that loss
Of joy that coming down brings she complained,
"It's not fair. Why's it me who had to doss
Down on my own while Mandi got to shag?"
Now, we all know the average sleeping bag

Is hard put to accommodate a pair,
Let alone three, but where there is a will…
 Donny, well-mannered, always glad to share,
Welcomed and comforted poor Candi till
She was as satisfied as Mandi, There
The trio lay in blissful slumber, still
As a millpond, even stiller I'd dare say.
Not waking till the dawn of the new day.

Meanwhile what of the other two? I guess
You're asking. Curiosity, dear reader,
For all the cats it's killed is nonetheless
A healthy thing. I've always been a pleader
For knowledge over nescience, I confess.
And ever since Zeus had it off with Leda
The world has always loved to hear a story
Which dealt in depth with exploits amatory.

Suffice to say that Brandi and the captain,
Having collapsed onto a for'ard berth,
Had spent a pleasant night all tightly wrapped in
Each other's various limbs. There was no dearth
Of squeals of joy. The query one is apt in
Such a case to pose, *viz* "Did the earth
Move for you?" is one that surely oughta
Be seen as figurative; they were on water.

The next few days and nights were spent in much
The same way, though the combinations altered:
Sunbathing, coke, a sip of rum or such.
The girls' only complaint: the wind and salt'd
Make their skin less than perfect to the touch.
In rectifying this Don never faltered.
His hands kept busily applying lotion;
The rest of him was peaceful as the ocean.

But oceans are not always full of peace.
Strong winds can whip up waves that toss and rock
A craft until its crew plead for release
From violent movement. Gales can pound and knock
Even the sturdiest vessel. When they cease
The damage done can sometimes be a shock.
Just such a gale arising quite a stir made
Among those sailing on the *Biped Mermaid*.

"Fear not," said Randy. "This will soon abate.
We'll ride it out. This yawl is built so well
There's not a storm could incapacitate
Her. She's sailed through the hell
Of Cape Horn waters, even through Bass Strait.
Why this is nothing: just a moderate swell."
But as he spoke the spinnaker was shredded.
A broadside spun her from where she'd been headed.

Donny suggested hauling in the sails.
Randy, high on coke, said, "I'll be damned!
This is what sailing's all about!" The rails
Were by now dipping under as she slammed
From side to side. Then the horrendous gale's
Fury was joined by rain. The women scrammed
Under the canvas housetop. There they cowered,
Certain the Mermaid would be overpowered.

And through all this, what of the vessel's skipper?
Was Randy standing steadfast in command,
Despite not feeling (like them all) too chipper?
Well, frankly, no. But you must understand
He thought the thought of sinking with his ship a
Concept overrated and he planned
If things got really bad then the best thing he
Could do would be to launch the pulpit dinghy

With just himself, one other and the coke.
Which other? That was but a small dilemma.
Candi or Mandi? Brandi or the bloke?
Any of them would suit his stratagem, a
Plan indeed which virtue loving folk
might harshly judge. I'm loath, though, to condemn a
Fellow man for cowardice or greed.
Morally we are each a thin, frail reed.

The waves (though "waves" seems too benevolent
A word) rose halfway up the mast then crashed
Onto the *Mermaid's* deck. The air was rent
Not only with the screaming winds that smashed
the rigging and the dinghy, and that sent
Overboard anything that wasn't lashed
Down tightly (and some that were lashed, too)
But also with the cries of all the crew.

For hours that seemed like days, for days that seemed
Like months, the storm tossed the poor yawl about.
With every thunderclap somebody screamed.
With every lightning bolt you'd hear a shout.
No nightmare Donny Johnny'd ever dreamed
Had terrorised him so. There was no doubt.
The motor, lights, pump, radio all gone,
He knew they'd be but briefly hanging on.

Too late by far for Randy's planned escape,
The stricken *Biped Mermaid* seemed just like
Fay Wray when in the grip of that great ape
Atop the Empire State. No use to psych
Oneself up against this force. No scrape
He'd ever been in had been known to strike
Such dread and panic into Donny's heart.
Then one freak wave smashed the poor craft apart.

Donny lost consciousness. When he came to
He found himself clutching a water tank,
Half empty, floating under a sky so blue,
So bright, the storm quite spent, while of the Yank,
There was no sign, nor any of his crew.
He could not see even a single plank
Of the poor *Biped Mermaid*. On each side
The Indian Ocean spread, serene and wide.

At least he had some water. For how long
He could survive was anybody's guess.
The sun was blistering. What else could go wrong?
Despair could be expected. Nonetheless,
Our hero's optimism was so strong
That even these dire straits could not depress
His spirits. His water tank, as you will note,
Was half-*full* and it doubled as a boat!

Now you or I, dear reader, would have thought
The situation hopeless, cast adrift
To be the waves', the winds', the currents' sport,
But "seek and ye shall find;" he had the gift
Of hope, so, squinting in the sun, he sought
Some vessel that might offer him a lift
And saw, on the horizon, a small dot
That might, just *might*, have been another yacht.

The dot grew, coming straight for Donny Johnny,
It surely was a boat, not just a piece
Of flotsam or some bird. Now, all doubts gone, he
Waved in its direction. Sweet release
From Neptune's clasp was close. The sun still shone. He
Was sure they'd see him, sure that soon he'd cease
This lonely bobbing on the ocean, soon
Have other humans with whom to commune.

It was indeed a vessel, some small trawler,
Fishing, perhaps. He cared not from where.
The gap between it and him grew smaller
Until it drew alongside and a pair
Of figures at the gunwale waved. A call, a
Hoarse reply from Donny, and then there
He was, wet, hungry, weary, but on board.
His spirits, never low, now truly soared.

His rescuers appeared to speak a tongue
Which Donny did not know, had never heard.
These kindly foreign sailors who had sprung
Him from the jaws of death said not a word
That he could understand: not one among
Those gathered round him. Donny, undeterred,
With smiles and gestures showed his gratitude,
Also his rather pressing need for food.

And then from somewhere near the vessel's stern
He heard a voice call, "English do you speak?"
A female voice. Donny could just discern
A group: the old, the very young, the weak,
The female, huddling there. "I try to learn,"
The voice continued. Eyes downcast and meek
Beneath a hijab, did not meet his, yet
He felt their unseen beauty, black as jet.

"My name is Donny Johnny, what is yours?"
"Fawziah," came the answer. Then she looked
Up briefly at him. "I am here because
I pay much money." "Lady, you've been rooked,"
Thought Donny, looking round. After a pause
She went to speak again. Our hero crooked
His finger, beckoning her closer. She
Stayed put. "I am, how you say, refugee."

So that explained their miserable state.
There must have been some sixty of them squeezed
Into a space where maybe seven or eight
Could comfortably fit. The frail, diseased
And kids among them accounted for a great
Percentage. Had they all somehow displeased
Their countries' leaders to the point where flight
Was now their only option? It's not right.

These were the thoughts that spun in Donny's head.
To his gratitude was added pity.
At brute injustice he always saw red,
And felt for victims no matter what the city
Or village they were from. Fawziah said,
"I am from Kabul." "I have heard of it," he
Replied. "Why did you have to leave?" "I fought
For the interests of the girls I taught. "

Donny thought Fawziah's English fine,
Though not the very finest thing about her.
Her smile and how it made her black eyes shine:
Little could top that, but without a doubt her
Sad plight affected him. "What philistine,"
He wondered, "Could so cruelly put to rout a
Teacher just because she took a stand
For her girl students? What a stupid land!"

"The others," Donny waved in their direction.
"Why are they fleeing? Are they Afghan too?"
Fawziah shrugged. It seemed she'd no connection
With any of the others, never knew
Their origins. A miserable collection
Of sad humanity they were, and that is true.
Just then a thin hand suddenly descended
On Donny's shoulder and this chat was ended.

By gestures it was made perfectly clear
That adult males on board had their own space.
Women and kids were crowded in the rear
Whilst men had commandeered the for'ard space,
What's more (and this gave Donny J no cheer)
Gazing on Fawziah's pretty face
Was not approved of by those in command.
He'd best be patient until they reached land.

The captain of this oddly peopled craft
Was called Suyadi. Dour-faced and devout,
He made it clear the whole boat, fore and aft,
Was his domain without the slightest doubt.
Apart from him the boat was only staffed
By one young lad, smiling, brown and stout,
"Ali," he said, tapping his own chest, and,
"Bali," to indicate his native land.

Donny feared his half-full water tank
Was the sole reason he'd been hauled on board.
Their own supply was very low. They drank,
And ate some boiled rice rationed from a hoard
Which Suyadi controlled. Our hero shrank
From thoughts of just what might have been. Restored
In spirits by this meagre meal, however,
He gave thanks to his stars or to whatever

Gods may be presiding over fate.
He rather thought there were none, but was smart
Enough to know he must impersonate
A Muslim now, and that when they took part
 In prayers, he should seem to participate.
He'd be mad to upset this applecart.
He watched Suyadi lay out on the deck a
Prayer mat and kneel on it, facing Mecca.

At least he faced the stern, so Donny Johnny
Assumed the holy city of the Hadj
Lay behind them somewhere, whereupon he
Knelt likewise, having made sure Ali's large
Buttocks hid any *faux pas*. Off and on he
Glanced up (unseen by the man in charge,
He hoped) to see if he could spot Fawziah.
Alas, it was impossible to see her.

A few days passed, all of them uneventful.
Then one calm evening, soon after dusk,
To Donny's nose a half-forgotten scent, full
Of earth with a slight harshness like the husk
Of coconut or bark, came. Not resentful
In the least (though he'd prefer the musk
Of female flesh) he knew that he was smelling
The journey's end. What next? There's no foretelling.

Suyadi cut his engine, coasted in
To a small creek, then Ali tossed the anchor.
One of the men jumped overboard. His chin
Was just above the water line, the bank a
Metre or so away. He flashed a grin
That glowed in the night sky. Now any rancour
Donny might have felt towards Suyadi
Dissolved. This whole adventure was foolhardy,

But worth it just to see that fellow grinning,
Happy to touch ground in a foreign land
After who knows what hell, but he was winning,
His broad smile gave Don to understand,
His freedom and a glorious new beginning
Awaited him, awaited the whole band.
Donny was next to jump into the water;
The other passengers were somewhat shorter.

They climbed over the gunwale one by one.
Donny and his friend grabbed hold of each.
Then, giggling as if this were just for fun.
They were set down upon a tiny beach.
With this disembarkation fully done
Suyadi left. It took two steps to reach
The shore, where Donny chose at once to steer
Straight for a rock upon which sat Fawziah.

They looked into each other's eyes. They sighed.
Was it just relief that made them do so?
You, reader, may think otherwise, and I'd
Hazard that you'd not be Robinson Crusoe
In thinking that, but they were dignified
And did not let their baser feelings loose, oh
Dear no, not here, for as you'd expect,
They showed their fellow travellers that respect.

"Suyadi said we wait here till someone
Comes to pick up us," Fawziah said.
"But I not trust him. I think we must run."
Donny had heard stories of people led
To parlous ends by swindlers, and thought none
Of Suyadi's ilk worth trusting. If ahead
Lay the wrath of angry immigration
Cops then this was far from a salvation.

They stole away and found a kind of cave
Which gave them shelter and some privacy.
Fawziah said, "I am no longer slave
To Muslim customs," and dramatically
Threw off her hijab, letting wave on wave
Of raven hair fall, tumbling, shining, free.
There's nothing quite as sensual as hair,
Say some, dear reader, be it dark or fair.

They sat together in that cave a while
Telling each other of their histories.
Donny, transfixed by Fawziah's sweet smile,
Often lost track. Forgetfulness would seize
His brain, as if his memory's data file
Had been deleted. Still, at times like these
It's wise to stem the flow of memory's fount.
Some chapters it were best not to recount.

Autobiography's a tiring game.
Soon all those words had wearied each pure mind.
They fell asleep. Now who am I to blame
Them if they woke next morn somewhat entwined?
Why, reader, if you think that there is shame
In such togetherness, it's you I find
Lacking in innocence. Suffice to say
They glowed as they woke to the dawning day.

As they surveyed the scene by morning's light
They saw the country's utter desolation.
All that met the eye to left or right
Was sand and rocks and scrubby vegetation.
Would death by thirst and hunger be their plight?
However sweet, you can't eat liberation.
While they were pondering how to survive,
They heard a heavy vehicle arrive.

Donny Johnny climbed a stony rise
And saw a truck and men in uniform.
"The immigration cops: that's no surprise,"
He thought. "They've been tipped off." He watched them swarm
Into the bush and heard the anguished cries
Of former shipmates. "That seems true to form
For Suyadi, that lowdown, scheming wanker,
Paid by both sides, just like a dodgy banker."

Having mused thus, our hero slid back down
The slope to where Fawziah waited, fear
And apprehension causing a deep frown
Which failed to mar her beauty. "Ah, my dear,
You'll understand I didn't nearly drown
To be arrested and imprisoned here.
We must lie low." He told her what he'd seen.
They piled some rocks to make a kind of screen.

She needed comforting. His arms were strong.
Need I, dear reader, tell you more than this?
The time till safety seemed extremely long.
Must I recount each soft caress, each kiss,
Each breathed endearment? No, it would be wrong.
Besides, I'm sure there's not too much amiss
With your imagination. Some hours passed
Until they judged that they were safe at last.

They vowed to brave whatever might impend.
Then, hand in hand, they timidly set out
In search of water, food, some kind of friend.
Heading inland, beset by fear and doubt,
Wondering just how this all would end.
They guessed the truck's tyre tracks would lead them out
To a road or some manifestation
Of what out here might pass for civilisation.

And so it did. Two lanes of sticky tar,
North-South: our Donny couldn't have been surer.
"We'll wait here for some passing truck or car,"
He said, thinking Fawziah's looks would lure a
Driver to stop. A van slowed down. Aha!
Success so soon! Its sign read "Aqua Pura
Swimming pool maintenance and cleaning service".
It pulled up. They approached, expectant, nervous.

"G'day. What's up?" This cheery salutation,
Followed by, "Where the bloody hell ya headin'?"
Drew from Donny J, "Our destination
Is Fremantle." "Well you're in luck. So, get in.
There's a bloody way to go." The pair's elation
Lessened when the driver ("Name's Mick") said in
His hearty voice, "I reckon you should keep
Me entertained or else I'll fall asleep.

"So tell me your story." Donny thought it wise,
Until he knew Mick better, to avoid a
Factual account. Let's face it, lies
Can make, if they're intelligently employed, a
Tale seem truer than when one applies
The facts. He sought not merely to embroider
The truth but to destroy it, thread by thread,
And weave a whole new fabric in its stead.

I shall not bore you, reader, with the details
Of DJ Donny's fabricated bio.
After all, you've had the truth from me. Tales
Fantastical, owing nought to Clio,
Have no appeal to one like me who retails
History unvarnished. I wouldn't even try, oh
No, to list his pseudo-souvenirs.
Suffice to say they left bluff Mick in tears.

"Jeez, mate, you've had it rough," was Mick's reply.
"I'd love to help you. Ever cleaned a pool?"
Donny said he'd give anything a try.
"Cash in hand," said Mick, "'s my general rule.
The taxman needn't know. You'll have to buy
Some clothes and tucker and I reckon you'll
Need somewhere to live." He reached into his pants
Pocket, pulled out some notes. "Here's an advance."

All that day and the next (with a brief stay
To grab some sleep at a third rate motel)
They travelled south and as they made their way
Mick explained to them how very well
Off were the residents of WA
(Apart from those who had been known to dwell
There for forty thousand years or more)
Thanks to the Chinese need for iron ore.

"There's suburbs full of multi-millionaires.
I've customers as rich as all get-out.
They're always looking for housemaids, *au pairs*
and so on. Your missus there, no doubt,
Could get a job as well. Then all your cares
Money-wise would just go walkabout."
Wiping the arses of their bratty kids
Or polishing their pure gold dustbin lids

Did not appeal to Fawziah but she
Kept her counsel. They arrived in Perth,
Spent the night chez Mick, then cheerfully
Just as the sunrise heralded the birth
Of a new day, boss and employee
Set off, knowing that there was no dearth
Of pools that they could make to look just so
In Dalkeith, Mosman Park or Cottesloe.

Mick did the rounds of his rich clientele,
Introducing Donny as he went.
Each mansion seemed to have a tale to tell,
A tale of grotesque taste, of millions spent
On sheer vulgarity and size. Could those who dwell
Among such ostentatious ornament
Be normal humans, Donny asked himself,
Or freaks engendered from excessive pelf?

Next day our hero drove the van around
While Mick stayed home and did the books. By four
O'clock that sultry afternoon he found
Himself knocking at the tradesmen's door
Of some *faux château* that would confound
The aesthetics of Graceland mixed up with décor
By Saddam, all in aqua, gilt and mauve,
The tackiest house in all of Peppermint Grove.

There was no answer, but from by the pool
A sozzled voice called, "Here!" so Johnny turned
And there, on a chaise longue, clutching a cool
Long glass of something pink, could be discerned
The lady of the house. The born-to-rule
Peremptoriness that comes from wealth unearned
Was clearly in her voice; that single word
Was quite enough to show it, even slurred.

"You've come to clean the pool, I gather... Wow!"
She looked him over, squinting in the sun.
"Come closer. Hmm. I like what I see. Now
Take your shirt off. Not just anyone
Can clean my pool. You realise I allow
Myself some extra service, just for fun.
You get my drift?" Donny stood, perplexed,
Wondering what on earth would happen next.

"The maid has quit. There's no-one here but us.
I'm Jeannie, by the way, but you can call
me Madam or Ms Rhinestone. Let's discuss
What other small, or maybe not so small
Jobs I might give you." Then, with no more fuss
than if she brushed a leaf that dared to fall
nearby, she dropped her swimsuit top and flung
Her arms wide. "Now, let's see how well you're hung."

Donny thought fast and came up with a plan.
"You need a maid. My girlfriend needs the work.
I'll call her now. My phone is in the van."
He turned and, with the thought that, "There's one perk
I can do without," once out of sight he ran.
But Jeannie Rhinestone's not someone you irk
Without reprisal. She picked up her Nokia,
Rang Mick and said, "Your contract's looking rockier.

"That's three men in a row who've turned me down.
You'd better hurry and send someone new
Or I'll make sure there's no pool in this town
You'll ever clean again. I'm warning you.
I need a stud, not some pathetic clown.
Meanwhile come here yourself. You'll have to do."
Donny worked the next few hours in fear;
He couldn't wait to get back to Fawziah.

Mick, looking worn out, met him at the door.
"Strewth, mate, I've got bad news. The Immigration
Came round just as I got home. I saw
Them take Fawziah for interrogation.
Jeannie Rhinestone's fixed this up, I'm sure.
What she says goes. She runs this bloody nation.
You knocked her back, which put her in a shit,
So she's found out Fawziah's not legit."

Donny was downcast. Donny's tears were shed
To think of what awaited that brave soul
Back in a land where ten-year-olds were wed
To whom their parents chose, and where control
By males was rarely challenged. She had fled
From what seemed like some archaic black hole
Where ignorance, misogyny and fear
Held sway, and now, to be sent back! Fawziah!

He wept. He sobbed. He called himself a twit.
He cursed the gods. He cursed his lack of thought.
He told himself he should have grabbed a bit
Of what La Rhinestone offered. Well, distraught
As he now was, and with the benefit
Of hindsight he could say, "Of course I ought
To have done such and such," but at the time
Resisting Jeannie seemed far from a crime.

Reflect a while, dear reader, on the fact
That whilst Afghanistan was thought to be
An unsafe place where Taliban attacked
With suicide bomber and with IED,
Whose own police and military lacked
The wherewithal to keep their people free
From violence, yet on the other hand
It was considered just the kind of land

Which people like Fawziah could be sent
Back to. The logic seems to fail, but I
Have never had the kind of mind that's meant
For logic, so it's best we say goodbye
To musings of the kind. It's time we went
Back to where DJ was heard to cry,
"Oh, woe is me! Poor, dear Fawziah! Woe!
Woe, that I ever saw that *faux château!*"

He carried on like that for half a day,
But there were pools to clean and cash to earn.
And though he never would forget the way
His dear Fawziah'd been made to return
He got on with his life and, shall we say,
With effort overcame the urge to spurn
The multitude of women, semi-clad,
Who lounged beside the pools. Was that so bad?

His skill at doing what pool cleaners do
Was such that soon his fame spread far and wide.
Mick's business consequently grew and grew.
He put on extra staff and so supplied
The needs of pools and of their owners too
From Mandurah to Yanchep where beside
Each pool the smiles of every bathing beauty
Were proof of how Mick's staff performed their duty.

After some months when little changed at all,
Donny, still haunted sometimes by the spectre
Of Jeannie, whom he tried not to recall,
Felt his efforts for the service sector
Of Perth's economy begin to pall.
Unlike the bee, who never tires of nectar,
He found the lifestyle of this lotus-land,
Like its inhabitants, a tad too bland.

Sydney beckoned. To himself he said, "I
Must see what lies on this land's other shore.
He bade the West adieu and caught the redeye,
Flying into the great unknown once more
Like Captain Cook or some crusading Jedi,
Although without the same *esprit de corps*.
Eager to learn what hedonism could teach,
He first of all set out for Bondi Beach

Where surf and sand and beauty were displayed.
He found himself a flat. The rent was dear;
That's how it is in Sydney, I'm afraid.
One evening he dropped in for a beer,
Into his local, where bands often played.
He sat down with his drink in time to hear
The MC say, "Let's big it up with feelin'
For our next act. It's Ken. He's from New Zealan'."

The isles of Peace, the isles of Peace,
Those nuclear-free though shaky isles
Where Beauty's in the snowy fleece
Of ewes and their seductive smiles,
Where glacier'd mountain ranges rise
As massive as netballers' thighs:

Yes, Ao Tearoa, land
Of flightless birds and malformed vowels
So difficult to understand,
Where churnings of Earth's molten bowels
Can smash down cities, maim and kill,
Although I've left, I love her still.

And yet, sad as it is to say,
Despite the joys of Marlborough plonk,
Of pinot noir and chardonnay,
Of pinot gris and savvy blanc,
I'm prey to fits, not of *grand mal*, d'ya
Know, but of the worst nostalgia.

For I'm stuck here across the ditch
On the West Island (as it's known)
Scratching my nostalgic itch
Until it bleeds. Why do I moan?

Because, as you may be aware,
There are no bloody jobs back there.

The geysers still perform their trick.
Hot mud bubbles plop and burst
At Rotorua, but clever-dick
Economists have done their worst.
The Bay of Plenty's now a bay
Of pretty close to sweet FA.

When Reagan, Thatcher and their sort
With neo-liberal, *laissez-faire*
Advisors in the Eighties wrought
Havoc on workers everywhere,
Before their mayhem had begun
They chose NZ for a dry run.

Earthquakes that cause the soil, once hard,
To liquefy, dumped Aussie cheese,
French nuclear tests in her backyard,
We will not think of themes like these.
New Zealand has withstood them all,
Even that sneaky underarm ball.

Though 'Rogernomics' was all bunk,
It did what nothing else could do.
Much more than *Rainbow Warrior's* sunk,
The dollar's par with the razoo.
The Tasman's now a sea too far.
Dash down yon glass of pinot noir.

Thus sang, or would, or could, or should have sung
This Kiwi troubadour. DJ was gallant.
Nothing but words of praise came from his tongue,
Although the merest modicum of talent

Was all Ken showed. He's surely not among
(Besides, that accent is so damned repellant.)
The greatest that his homeland has let go,
Like Eric Beach, Ruth Park or Russell Crowe.

Ken proved, however, friendly, so they shared
A wine or two or three and got to chatting
On subjects ranging from the gigs they'd snared
To politics and Stephen Fleming's batting.
No cricketer's good name was that night spared,
Not even Hadlee's. Then Ken, thickly plaiting
His words and spilling his glass of Secret Stone,
Said, "My dad owns a nightclub, *Chez Capone*.

"His regular DJ has got the clap
Or some such untoward indisposition.
They need someone and you seem like a chap
Who's heaven-sent to take on the position.
What say tomorrow night you fill the gap?
I guarantee I'll get my dad's permission."
They shook, swapped numbers, left and the next day
Ken rang to say his father'd said OK.

Chez Capone, it seems, was all the rage
That month and might well be for weeks to come.
Fashions for clubs in our impatient age
Rarely endure. Some go broke and some
Fall victim to the turn of fashion's page
For no apparent reason. Well, the thumb
Of modish judgment howsoever earned
For *Chez Capone* was clearly upwards turned.

Donny had heard of many a violent fight
In Aussie nightclubs and in streets nearby.
But Ken assured him *Chez Capone*, despite

Its name, was peaceful as a butterfly.
In fact, he said, the venue's a delight
For punters who are very quiet and shy.
They're safe at *Chez Capone*. What really cheers 'em
Is its huge Maori bouncer, mean and fearsome.

That night, 'round ten, Donny set out on foot
Through Paddo and the Cross towards the city,
Observing as he went sights that would put
To shame the sets of movies known as "gritty".
If morals were colours, Sydney'd be as soot,
Although the Bridge is fine, the harbour pretty.
Quite soon, within a quarter-hour or less,
He'd reached what Ken had said was the address.

He thought himself the victim of some prank.
This surely was no entertainment zone.
A building that once might have been a bank
Back in the days when banks were made of stone,
Its windows blocked, its whole exterior blank,
Was this the famous club, the Chez Capone?
Then he saw the neon, blinking blue,
And up a side lane an extensive queue.

Donny proceeded to this long line's head
And there, behind a length of velvet rope,
A giant, just as Kiwi Ken had said,
Stood guard. There wouldn't be the slightest hope
Of getting past this model of NZ
Musculature. You'd have to be a dope
To even try. Donny had never seen
So much muscle with a face so mean.

Our hero, after one deep breath to quell
His apprehension, made his business clear.

The bouncer spoke into his left lapel
And looked back up with something very near
A smile, a look that would do just as well
To frighten as to be a cause for cheer,
Jerking his thumb towards the interior's murk.
So Donny Johnny went in to start work.

Backstage he found a library of old vinyl,
From '50s rockabilly to the Clash.
The kind of hoard that I wish had been mine, all
Waiting to be mixed—hip-hop and thrash,
Ballads and bubblegum. He made his final
Choice, including even Johnny Cash.
Then, as the punters filled the dim-lit space,
He socked it to 'em with more bass than grace.

He mixed and scratched and spun from this weird list
To a relentless beat. Zydeco, raga,
Tex-Mex and reggae, everything was grist
To Donny's pounding mill. While Bundy, lager
And alcopops were flowing, all those pissed
Young things shimmied to bits of Lady Gaga
Fused with the Stones and even the Big O
In DJ Donny Johnny's greatest show.

There was a break (Such things, I'm told, occur
From time to time in gatherings like this.)
From the sound's bewildering, rhythmic blur.
Even DJs need to take a piss
Occasionally, visit a masseur
Or change a sweaty outfit, though they miss
The adoration of the pulsing throng
And so they never leave the desk for long.

While Donny Johnny took a welcome swig
Of water (Well, there was no chardonnay
Mentioned in his rider and the gig
Was causing him to sweat in the worst way.)
A female punter, eyes so very big,
Trim, tanned, blonde, cute and quite décolletée ,
Came up and leaned across the desk and said,
"I'm Lara. Would you like to come to bed?

"No man I've shagged has been known to complain.
Or come into the loo and snort a line?"
"Why, thank you, miss. I'll pass on the cocaine.
I've given up the powder, but for mine
The first option is one I'll entertain.
A blowjob in the toilet would be fine."
Lara bridled. "Hmmph. Blowjob my arse!
I'll have you know I am a girl with class."

Donny apologised for his faux pas.
And Lara's anger seemed to be assuaged.
He spun a final set, his repertoire
Expanding as the drunken clubbers raged.
 Finished at last, he headed for the bar
When Lara reappeared. Our hero gauged
From her demeanour that she was prepared
To let bygones… Then Donny stopped and stared.

Two chaps, not quite yet men, no longer boys,
The kind who seem to have less brain than muscle,
Who, even sober, would be lacking poise,
Shoved each other, fell, began a tussle,
Their bodies rolling on the floor, the noise
Of fabric tearing heard above the hustle
Of last drink orders, girlish screams and clicking
Cameras, skin abraded, feet a-kicking.

He realised that it was on for real
When he saw a knife make ineffectual stabs.
If, in a brawl, I see a flash of steel
I'm out of there quicker than Ali's jabs
It's straight to Macca's for a Happy Meal
Or, better still, the Lebo's for kebabs.
Junk food is great to calm the frightened mind
And leave all thoughts of sudden death behind.

But Donny Johnny's made of sterner stuff
And he had Lara hanging off his arm,
So where I'd do a bunk he came on tough
And in a voice both menacing and calm
Said, "OK you two. Now that's quite enough.
I'll call the bouncer." Panic and alarm
Suffused the faces of the brawling pair.
Testosterone dissolved into thin air.

Such was the Maori man-mountain's repute
That no-one wanted him in the equation.
With peace, and Lara most impressed to boot,
The time had come for her kind invitation
To be accepted. All that was in dispute
Was that perennial question of location:
"Your place or mine?" Hers was closer by,
And so they stepped out under the dawning sky.

A mere two city blocks, albeit across
Some pools of vomit, the odd prostrate form
Of weary reveller and assorted dross,
The night's detritus, very much the norm
These days when "having a good time" means loss
Of consciousness, then, though a perfect storm
Of drugs and booze has finally prevailed,
You've neither been hospitalised nor gaoled,

And they were at the door of Lara's flat.
She fumbled with the key, he with the hook-
And-eye that held her tiny dress, whereat,
Having both succeeded, they both took
A tumble, tripping over the doormat
And her descending garment, then they shook
With laughter as they lay upon the floor
Entangled, each unwilling to withdraw.

They helped each other stand, each body leaning
Into the other, for balance and from lust,
And then collapsed again, after careening
Towards her bed, on which they landed, just.
They next proceeded, if you get my meaning,
To parry like fencers, with less cut than thrust.
Modesty, as you've no doubt surmised,
Was not a virtue Lara greatly prized,

But you and I, dear reader, aren't like that.
And so we'll draw a modest veil athwart
The next half hour or so. Then, rat-a-tat!
There came a sudden knocking. Donny thought
The wreckers were demolishing the flat,
So loud it was. Lara, quite distraught,
Whispered, "The wardrobe, quick !" There Donny sped,
Kicking his clothing underneath the bed.

Lara unlatched the door. He dared to peer
Through a small crack to see who'd come to visit.
What met his eye caused him the greatest fear
He'd ever known. With terror quite exquisite
He wished that he could somehow disappear
Completely. Now it isn't common, is it,
To crouch, nude, in a lady's wardrobe, while
She entertains? At least it's not my style.

But what made Donny's state the worst of all
As he continued in that 'robe to skulk
Was that he recognised who'd come to call.
Only one man had such impressive bulk.
It was the nightclub bouncer, eight feet tall
And twice the width of the Incredible Hulk.
With direst panic DJ's heart was gripped
To see his muscles ripple as he stripped.

Lara and her visitor, alack,
retired to bed. Vain thought that she'd dismiss him.
As Donny watched them through that tiny crack
He winced to note the heat with which she'd kiss him.
Then, as they made the "beast with double back",
He wondered if she'd staged the scene to piss him
Off as payback. Whether or not, "It's clear,"
He thought. "I really must get out of here."

When finally, their sweet exertions ended,
The pair were filling up that small apartment
With a duet of snores, why only then did
Our hero, knowing what "a pounding heart" meant,
With first one hesitant, light foot extended,
Then his whole naked self, knew to depart meant
The risk of being caught, but that to stay
Meant he would never see another day.

His clothes were irretrievable. To reach
Beneath the lovers' bed where they were stashed
Would likely wake the giant. He kept each
Slight movement minimal. An idea flashed
Into his mind (Dear reader, I beseech
You not to judge him; he was quite abashed.
Morality dissolves when panic presses.)
He'd help himself to one of Lara's dresses.

Thus clad he crept out to the city street,
A busy one. The sun by now was high.
He'd left his phone behind, so could not tweet
For help, but not one single passer-by
(This being Sydney) thought him ought but sweet
(Lara always dressed to please the eye.)
He got back to his residence. No key,
No card, no cash, no clothes: a quandary.

Luckily, the landlord lived downstairs
And was a pleasant fellow—a rare breed,
The pleasant landlord—so, thinking his cares
(The worst of them, at least) were gone indeed,
He knocked and, muttering to himself some prayers
For understanding in his hour of need,
Said, "I've been in a closet. Now I'm free."
The landlord looked him over. "So I see."

from *Taking Queen Victoria to Inveresk* (1997)

Fruit and Flowers

Still life? At first only the frame sings with the zing
of fruit, pours its juice of light into one corner,
to sustain objects detached from sap,
cut and culled away from life to art.

The optimistic English translates to French
as *nature morte*, dead fruit still edible,
dead blooms still fresh with garden colour.
At what stage do picked things die, become
art, decoration, food? If there's no heart, no brain
to stop, what's the point
at which only the artist can save an inert bunch
from being dead boring?

Why, for that matter, do we say "dead boring"
as if death did not fascinate us
at least as much as art and life
and almost as much as where they interface?

A ranunculus is a ranunculus is . . .
as Stein could have said (but didn't,
roses being more accessible and more
euphonic), and people who like paintings of flowers,
Cocteau said, love flowers and hate art.

But the painted image of a stem
is not a stem, as those old modernists
should have known (*"Ceci n'est pas une pipe."*)

The aim was not to elicit saliva or tears,
for the peaches trying not to look
too human and indelicate, almost succeeding,
nor for Sweet Williams like targets but not quite dead centre.
(That's called "interesting composition" and shows
the artist was "imaginative".)

Still less for strawberries, one up, one down,
like the masks that advertise amateur dramatics
in 1850 drawing rooms, or like
the terrace houses of the working class.
Half ripe, if bitten they would only yield
the sweeter, livelier part, nearer the base,
once the tough tip had been spat out.

Nor were we meant to drool
for gooseberries veined like a pair of eyes,
grapes black and white with hyacinths to match,
an idealist's symmetry of seasons.

These are rather foods and flowers for thought,
for meditating on the best of both worlds,
both dimensions of the framed plane, dark and bright,
swinging on the century's hinge, still and alive.

Sunday in the Gardens

Little Miss Licorice Legs, fling the sky today,
lob the sunlight up behind the hedge
and let it bounce where the smallest dancing kids
are no more than extra dapples,
a blossom froth of muslin.

Today the future doesn't bulk
like nursemaids dull as duty. Not yet
will a gent, the cut of his coat a dance itself,
try to win your smile from beneath a flowered hat.
Today it's a gift to the air.

The garden steps are stripes of sun.
They lead up from innocence.

Naming the Sensation No 2

"Girls just want to have fun."
   — Cyndi Lauper

Rothko died from an overdose
of mystic seriousness and Clyfford Still
rode, lone, the rim of his own spirit's ranch.

JP, of course, romanticised
biochemistry and his muscles,
mistaking both for power, got it wrong.

Barney Newman won the Cold War,
his stripes like a sergeant's or a flag's,
art's own John Wayne in Sensurround.

Motherwell can't place quite all
the blame on Freud, who taught him that
boys just want to have angst.

Paint as bourbon, semen, sweat,
the quest, the thrust: the galleries
confused testosterone with art.

Half of humanity meanwhile
was object, suffixed by De Kooning's
Roman numerals, or hid outside

the rich white cube of fame, head down,
bum up and waiting, either for or on.
Now at last we all can see

the world through rosy TV screens,
more *Rage* than rage, a festival
of clips and chats, layers of cathode pink

as taffeta, lip gloss giving lip,
a nub of candy in the purse, the pulse
engulfing, innermost delight.

from *New Foundations* (1976)

Autumn

I. Behind the Phoenix Foundry

Mallarmé's curse rides over Launceston.
Autumn sticks to the foundry yard.
This morning had the old trick in it:
the air virgin, dry,
pretending cleanliness.

What is tempting now
is the easy elision, the colour-coded sketch:
to surround the sonnet with absence
like a page.

Let the hero go spinning out into his margins.
Open the tombs.
Observe the chemistry of after-death:
nitrogen, seepage, the skilled craft
of bacteria.

The racks of angle-iron are bright
with flux. Oxygen creates
these orange flakes. Real gases
control the world. Two kids
play here, off the street, safe,
in harmony with the tough scrap.

II. Fisherman

Where is the old stability?
The dinghy wobbles on the ebb.
Who will come home
past the long island?
(Eucalypts stand green.)
No-one coughs blood. This is not Valvins.

Through the heads with the tide:
one, singing at the tiller,
shirtless impresario,
burnt against the clouds?
Idle speculation.
Thank god and Dampier our swans are black.

III Against Mallarmé

This is a canny pioneer country.
The trees stay the same colour
until they're scrubbed and
trucked and chipped and sold.
The unnerving smell of the bush
has been a challenge to the genius of man
for cyclic comfort. Man,
on his own terms, wins, and gets
Pinus radiata where birds don't go.

Even while the mist of fish blood
spreads, "effulgent haze", from
the hard hope of the knife,
the fisherman knows
that one day the catch will be
something stranger even than his song.

A leaf from an imported tree
falters, then settles.

The kids are called in to the terraces.
An absence of their playing remains.

The poem, however, refuses to hang about,
will neither be caught nor rust,
is not dependent on seasons,
but is being forged

in the haul, in the furnace,
the real grave and the game.

from *Five Trees*

Acacia Melanoxylon

When they found old Terry he'd been dead for a week.
There was no garden to speak of round his shack,
but in the front paddock stood a mighty blackwood
symmetrical and pure. Driving past,
you couldn't take your eyes off it.

                              Blackwood,
the most beautiful of trees.

                         It was the Rigby boys
who found him. Shook them up a bit, they said.
They buried him down in the town cemetery.
Should've put him under that blackwood, I said.

There was no glass in either of his windows.
He used to chuck his food scraps out of them
to feed the possums, rats and chooks.

Casuarina Stricta

The kids of the people we bought the house from
had a cubby-house of she-oak branches
up against the back fence. Only the funnel-webs
used it for a couple of years. Then I burned it down.
Took half the fence with it, but the tree
they'd ripped the branches from remained, surrounded
by black waste. There are patterns in its bark
which modulate into the fruiting cones.

It is important not to let the patterns break down.
The past must remain personal. It's complicated enough.

So when the rusty flowers fall, covering the ash,
there will be a basis. I won't have to let
the children or the spiders back in. I can live
my past out with the tree and stand
next to it and stand on the new soil.

Myoporum Insulare

The beach is asbestos. Here I will not burn.
In fact, the boobiallas and the railway line
have lost their link with light. Yesterday three bodies
were washed up, two small boys and a teenage girl,
all fully dressed, looking normal. The day before,
a young bloke in overalls. Today I'm waiting
for the score. I've chain-smoked, burying the butts
in the grey sand. The smell of the purple berries
is the smell of death now. The *Tasman Limited*
will come past in twenty minutes. When it does
I'll laugh. I haven't laughed for two days.

I would like to come here, under the boobiallas,
every day for a few hours

and watch the sea.

December; Palo Alto

The sycamores are empty nets
dragging the rain.
Their leaves skid like fish
on the wet road.

Today they brought Angela here
across the Golden Gate
with winter.

Somewhere between Waxahachie and Woonsocket

1

Somewhere between Waxahachie and Woonsocket
somebody dies. Cleanly,
something slides into a
life like a liquid into the
fuel tank of a Saturn.

Of course, it's never that simple
but the actions of twenty thousand everydays
are all timed keenly
by the blade in the brain
and are calculated for the big moon-shot.

Buried under the black wax soil
of the south-eastern quarter of the USA
there is a large computerised plant
where it all works.
Think of the potential there

for imagery — pocket watch
which is really a heart; the gold
of Fort Knox; the fallout shelter
beneath the White House; steam
issuing under the Oracle's tripod;

stainless steel hell; wonders of surgery.
But think, mostly, of what above all
this wired womb goes on
and what, at times on the conscious earth,
stops going on.

2

When my uncle died I was kind of
awkward; at twelve I was awkward anyway.
But after the first dislocation,
after the mystery of seeing
a grown man lie down and grunt
and piss himself in the middle of a ball game,
after Dad and Uncle Pat had come
to attend to whatever it is
that men attend to at such times,
I took my young cousins round to the back yard
and furiously played kick-for-kick with them
against the cement wall. I joked loudly.
They laughed. Then I caught cousin Libby's eye
through the dining-room window. I tried
to show her in one look
that I knew why she was crying
but that I had a job to do.

3

Watch out for the bare wire,
for the spark in the cracked socket.
Kneeling, you are vulnerable; down
by the skirting-board, aware
of the volume of the room behind you,
of the space you occupied standing.

A second ago you knew all
the secrets of power. The future
was clean as the moon.

The present moment is liftoff.

4

Memento mori. Don't forget
to keep the hatchet blade well waxed.
The skull serves as a paperweight
or a reminder of your next
appointment with the dentist. Buff
and rinse, the clean drill gets the last
of the dull clinging film right off.
Grin at the nurse.

                    But you know that rust
on the hatchet would be a different story.
Coating with wax will keep it away
(bone round the brain).

                    Memento mori.
But in the meantime avoid decay.

5

Transmission from the promised landscape:

to the memory of Jules Verne,
to the guiding electric prophecies:
while men forgot and turned to each other
we have been lifted up, surely,
ungainly hermits of the metal creed,
to the wilderness with our holy dependence
on the artifacts of progress.

Perhaps a future primitive generation
will worship that huge disc in the sky.
Meanwhile we shall keep the radio contact tight.

The sky is black.

6

Small neon fires light up the mouth
of the open street, glint on teeth
of stores and pool halls. My shoes grind
on the gravel, walking in no-man's-land.
I break a spent match and flick it down.
Across town I hear a siren moan.

Downstairs to the warm bar; the jukebox
winks its signals to the bottles and back.
It bounces Janis Joplin off
the pinball crash, the juiced laugh.
I'm coddled by fusing noise here.

Above the machines, in the blank air,
is the wholeness of the corpse in orbit
between the womb and the waxed hatchet.

from *A Nickel In My Mouth* (1979)

from Antarctica Poems

The Worst Journey In the World

Head in the block of ice
his balaclava had become,
Birdie almost complained
the third day of the blizzard
with no tent. Cherry, blind even
in England, in day, "just did
what he was told". Gentle Bill
who did not trust fit sailors
had chosen them. Five weeks
of black, of pain, tea, pemmican,
biscuits, a birdnesting spree,
thumping each other's limbs for hours
to free clothing enough for rest.

Was the orgy still on in the Hut?
Who danced the Lancers with Anton?
They had peaches with syrup.
They had colours.

                        Camped high
out on the moraine under Terror
three aristocrats on a graceful
romp in Hell, life an egg balanced
on the toes of the shuffling
amateur Empire, found the tent
—a stick in the wide fury of ice—
bore it, a relic, given.

The Emperor eggs, the absurd grails,
had no embryos, were no use
for advancing ridiculous theories.

80° 08' 1934

"May was a round boulder sinking before a tide."
— Richard E. Byrd

Carbon monoxide like an aurora
in my veins blinding the haemoglobin
until nerve-ends are pellets
of fierce drift, June 1st:
three months on the wrong side of the sun,
my heart like the skipping engine
in the tunnel, its exhaust rimed up,
sending the blank gas round again
dizzying me down to two red candles,
one in a cracked china holder,
the other planted in its own tallow,
I have the tiny data on a shelf
in the Escape Tunnel. I have jobbed
in the substance of truth.
If they should have to come for me . . .
I am a Virginian.
I am a thin flame drawn between two voids.

Onyx River

The river of remembering
runs where there is no ice,
where coal seams album
chronology of hot trees,
fossils and grains of pollen,
penguin bones, Devonian items.
Here the bloom of slime is a
wipe of origin again.
Bacteria shift in their thin
ritual in the tenuous soil.
An oasis of noise: stones
the sun ribs through water chatter,
melt puddles move, colour
of the first fish, of the always
sun and the lake takes
dead mountains down and, blue,
robs them with hope. *Again*
is the bludgeon of slight cells
against a continent.

Gardening is the Opiate of the Elite

A crisis of petals
leaves me out stupid
as a sparrow and sharply
jacking the hurt gravel.

They want to drown my hill
in sweet stormwater.
I'm planting natives against
the bronchial onslaught.

"If they can sell you the idea
of the supernatural,
they can sell you anything,"
O'Grady said

They sold me a suburb full
of irony, shares in a
medium alderman
and a gerrymandered garden.

But the problem persists:
Torres kneeling on one knee
only (to take aim),
Corrigan with the Huks.

Trigger spring. Terraced fire
proves little. Am I some
Xavier Herbert of the
avenues and crescents?

While maoists stain the wattle
I get my politics
from Einstein, my facts
from the *Business Age*,

my theory of aesthetic
from (don't wince) Stalin.
I should do something about that.
John Forbes is working on it,

and others, too; some who love me
will despair at the light conjuring
with the abyss, but
nothing I do can establish

a *meaningful relationship*
between the eternal smartarse
and the death of ideals.
One tyrant or another cues.

Another mattock-slice
of clay: the Trots are
tempting me again
with that pebble-clean path

back to the door. The slam
of a dry house waiting for
a gale deafens the garden
and the gardener is bell-jarred.

Thursday night raising funds
to buy a trampoline
for the convent school:
legs eleven! Is it not,

Brother McCarthy, the captain
of the school you're thinking of?
The *barrios* of Cali
are not so flexible.

What is of specific
concern now is the erosion
Like the will off flesh
topsoil sluices. Rocks we need.

A rectal infestation
of theists is eating
our appetites, our rocks.
(On this petrified sigh, man

is grounded, ground.) Build
a wall, where? a series
of walls. Here, and here, up
the slope. Start from the bottom.

The bottom was lost rains ago.
The convent school captain
is probably bouncing now,
unlost. The mattock springs from a root.

Vanzetti

The charge that smashed your nerve cells apart
had too much volume for your corpse to keep.
Nothing could earth it. From your violent start
like one of Galvani's frogs against the straps
it hopped the gap to where the crowds, deep
around the Charlestown jail, around the world,
were waiting, latent, for that spark. Perhaps
the State of Massachusetts when it hurled
its bolts at you thought that you were not
in contact, would, alone, absorb the lot.

The charge they hit you with, on the other hand,
you and Niccola, was absurdly light.
Murdering payroll guards for fifteen grand
is nothing to men who wanted the big haul:
not just the money but the means; who'd fight
not cops or even judges but the force
that owned those forces, lethal capital.
Wrong in law and fact, Thayer was right, of course,
to sentence you. Bourgeois justice in this case
would have been hindrance, but it knows its place.

The heaviest charge is what you've laid on us:
to keep transmitting those raw lovely volts
until they think we're all as dangerous
as you and Sacco. Who will then be shocked?
Meanwhile we insulate, check for shorts and faults
and grope for the master switch somewhere among
the bizarre trappings of the power that knocked
your body shuddering like a prophet's tongue
that's running on and down when all is said
but nothing done yet by the woken dead.

Waiting for Franco to Die

Cornford at Tierz: the new planet wheels
to Boadilla. Dust is what you
eat and are. Now after forty
spitting years the chips are scattered;
a new die sprinkles and spurts
through them.

                The coolest
of the barbarians is dying in the Prado.
Viva la muerte! The virgins of death
will be paraded again down the Calle
de la Princesa, black edges
trembling in the cold wind
of organic law.

                The ace up
for the Nation. At the end
of Castilian summer, the white dust
wet at last. *Mare, Mare, Mare,
Mare esta Llorando* and well
she might with Pius Pacelli long dead.

How long will the cube of bone
roll? Will it be the coming snow
or the next we dig through to claim
the buried nuns for dancing partners?
Die, Francisco, with the pain
of knowing the poets will be back.

from *Tense Mood and Voice (1969)*

Star

for Stephanie

Proem

1.
You laugh at me behind your face
and twist the last ace out of your frilly sleeve.
I lose. I leave.

2.
The prisoners exercise in cages,
insane, concentric cricket nets.
No-one rages. Everyone plots.

3.
There are many things I lack,
but I'll get my own back later on.
Just wait, baby, I'll learn
every trick in the book, fly-leaf to colophon.

Amphetamine hands will cover your eyes.
Scintillating fingernails will rip your lace,
but that will be only in your brain.
I'll come up from behind.
My mind will blow your mind,
baby.
And it won't be me but my poetry
that blows in your belly.

I shall walk for you,
walk through a continent of streets

yard by dry yard
and wet,
through a string of cities
avoiding the cracks
for your sake.
I shall make
each step in praise of you:
the slow blow,
the controlled explosion of your complexion
and your composure, the skilled destruction
of every plane and crease
in your photogenic face,
baby.

Sequence

Each separate town is slapped on the highway like
a hoarding, vulgar as a teenage laugh.
Milkbars, town hall, rec. and cenotaph,
two pubs with snooker tables, public dyke
— interior: pale green semigloss (by the shire)
and thick, white coin-scratch (by the Baptist choir).

Slogans and flags wave from each service station
like some third world republic crude with pride.
Deep in those shabby, chrome milkbars I've plied
the jukeboxes with dud coins to saturation
or in the soft air of the saloon bars
sent the reds spinning like unruly stars.

Bold in studded leather I've played it cool;
aphrodisiac hamburgers and cokes
have led to furtive, half-successful pokes
under the pine trees down behind the school.

Then always the big wheelspin, the muffler gone,
the next raw town to burn. Clear out. Move on.

Crystal Palace

Cock of so many country towns, so sure,
I, who have sent so many spherical phrases
rolling for fluke breaks over the green cloth,
rhymes dropping into sweet, symmetrical pockets,
I have felt the poem grabbing at my guts,
the pen in my hand like a cue nestling into chalk
smoothly, despite the heavy breathing. Calm,
I have planned to avoid the easy eight-ball image
and have had in my head all the relevant intricate angles.

But my bitch of a muse is in league with a hustler:
prick-teasing stocking-tops at the saloon door,
every trick of the slicker with brylcreem hair
taking the simple lair for a ride
inside the bars of the city I want to love.
(The cage is merely a pun, therefore a cage,
a trap for the simple lair on every page.)
I want to love the city. I want to screw
her rolling grey in the sun. I want to screw
her cheap in the night with her neon hair. I want
that girl on the bus, busting out of her skirt for it,
the break that never ends, the one two-bob
that keeps the jukebox going till it melts.

Why should I always be the simple lair?
Why should I always wear
my poems like a shoestring tie?
My hair
too long, my pimples pointing to the sky?

The sky, it is true,
is always Mitchell blue.
I don't know why.

(Beware
of anything they offer you.
Beware of the con-man's swy.
Take care in Sydney, yeah.
Ooh,
they're
sly.)

After the killing you can only grin,
walk out, walk home. Desire has been taken away
along with your roll. Hundreds of empty cars
move down the empty streets. You cannot fill
the city with your braggadocio.
The simple grin has its own cunning, slides
values around like sheets of paper, so:
"Put it all down to experience."
"Your father could have told you so."
A fool and his cliches soon are parted from
the truth. The truth is you are beaten, broke.
She's kicked you out with your balls in a fiery knot.
The ram slips sheepishly, lopsided, off.

(Avoid the grin
inevitably inane.
If you can't win,
then don't stick out your chin;
some bastard'll hit it again.
Pack in
the down-but-not-out, thin,
brave, callow grin.

Grab pain.)

Pain

1.
The street lies out, inviting,
the flat of a large-bladed knife.
Slap your soles on it, test its temper.
think of the edge, dwell on it, dwell on it.

There at the tip a street-light drips.
I think of all the vulnerable parts
of the human body, throat and wrists,
baby-soft hollows between ribs and hips.

2.
In my room I find twenty-one cents in change
scattered among the cheap, essential furniture.
It's nearly ten. It's worth the risk.
The pub is just two blocks away.

Calm down. Breathe slow and flex your fist.
Before I've finished my beer a drunk's thrown out
protesting. "But it's payday. I can pay!
Look!" I don't need to look. I follow him,

sure and dark, into a lane. "Got a light?"
One punch . . . a plastic wallet—twenty quid
and a crumpled photo of him with five kids.
Calm down. I suppose his wife works, anyway.

Envoi

Baby, I've shown you what I mean by art.
I've made it at last here on the big-town scene.
Sure, I've been conned and hustled but I'd been
too big too long back home. Look, kid, I'm smart.
I've got a ring with a real garnet and I wear
real sharp suits, dark socks. I know the score.
You won't be laughing at me any more.
You wouldn't recognise the country lair.
I realise now it wasn't only you
I had to get even with. I had to strike
back hard at all of them till I came through
with words that screamed louder than any bike,
louder than anything on the hit parade,
but true, but true. Baby, I've got it made.

from *The What of Sane* (1971)
Whatever Happened to Conway Twitty?

My bakelite mantle set pulled him in
through the whine and crackle of KZ and I
drummed on a dented pencil tin
to *Danny Boy* or *Mona Lisa*,
tensing my hands and jaw as his art
made seven syllables of "heart".

Five p.m. was too early to get
anything like a good reception
and I broke the volume knob off that set
trying to bring America closer,
or if not America, then at least
Stan the Man, oracle and priest.

Masturbation and vandalism
came with darkness, but first the radio
would spurt its sweet, commercial chrism,
the god would descend through static, lift up, up,
up to the top of the *Cashbox* chart
all seven syllables of my heart.

High Country

1. Homecoming

Button-grass flats, pale through the drizzle: my eyes
unhinged, unhinging; patch-brown pools:
my body's own still liquids.

After the climb, hard through the spine's country,
where the leatherwood and myrtle drip
holes into the bent flesh,

after the droplets running off the tight skin
around the vein-riddled gullies
stretched on a hairpin bend,

this is the homecoming, arriving at this level —
the brain laid open in the wet,
nerve ends like sags, open.

2. The Hut

The plastic strips flap in the doorway still,
sad alchemical colours to ward off evil.
The poet comes home like a blue-arsed fly
too late for the real summer, too soon
for the winds that take the corner of the year
on two loud tyres—the screech of March.

I light the fire and wait for my life's details
to dry out—buckled paperbacks,
the sleeve of an early Dylan record
(young jew-angel's face, cowboy mystery,
holding his guitar's neck like a flowering tree).

A man could die waiting between these hills.

Outside in gumboots, moving rocks around,
channelling off the water, watching it take
used-up petals like brain cells with it, down
to the flats where my brackish eyes are set like traps,
I am immune here, acting without itch,
connections all leached, open, waiting.
One day, too late for insects, bleak with peace,
after a month of my turning stones by the moon,
the hills will hear the brash harmonica
and send a patly scored reply in gusts.
And in that instant as the axis tilts
someone will cross the sags, his clothes blown dry.

Sideflower

Your highway body,
my love a sideflower
indigo-petalled like a
jealous kiss.

That married bastard mauled your
ringfinger.

I wore my red scarf over the Shoalhaven
and saw how sadly straight the
road was.

Man and Law

A milk-dipped finger points to trace
words on the table. Lacking grace
to speak his words against a tune,
he hides behind the afternoon.
Fingernails and cigarettes
suffer. The lines finished, he wets
his finger again. The words run
into each other. Outside, the sun
still drinks the suburb through a straw.
Hands are still weaker than the law.

"*O triste, triste était mon âme
à cause, à cause d'une femme,*"
he writes, forgets the rest. He who
would terrify the world has to
convince himself he is not sane,
obliterates the lines again.
From the bruised throat human pride
still bubbles like the day outside.
Self-imposed penances are for
those who understand the law.

So curse Verlaine with woman-kind.
A man should hide behind his mind
if anywhere. Rage. Rage. He tries,
but he can only terrorise
citizens with cups of tea
whose eyes are ordered not to see
the shame extending from his hands
back to the brain which still demands
strength against the open door
letting in sunlight like the law.

He leaves the table, walks across
to the door, breathes, knows his loss
more clearly by looking at his fists.
The shaft of golden dust persists.
The mess of milk on the table dries.
Soon the inexorable flies
will come. He steps into the yard.
The sun burns through the soft facade
of shame to uncover even more
strength than he needs to break the law.

from *The Atlas* (1982)

II

This, then, was the city.
I would learn to cope, slowly,

nursed in the sedulous old stone
mapped with mosses,

a huge cottage
nestled at the top dizzy

edge of its own stone's quarry, crazy
and soothing.

Upstairs lived the old woman
they said. Below

the quarry: the stone warehouses,
the harbour soft with yachts.

The narrow bakery
filled the lane air at night;

dully from the pubs and wharves thuds
of car-doors, cargo;

traffic was the unknown, the big
intersection was a cross for a country kid

in Battery Point, enclosed
by trucks and the bedless Derwent

where water slowly became alluvial silt,
thicker and warmer, down

to the earth's muddy core. Here, though,
was a village; the ways of strange adults

worked for me: a circle to
charm and cocker.

Each morning Dad would work
the Prefect across town

and out into where a thousand children
were tumbling, new,

the berry-orchard slopes
from thin houses.

I would stay.
The world of the old garden

rose around me. There were
cousins of some strange remove

to play with. They knew
about the city.

They went to a school that had uniforms,
carried books across the road;

one of them rode a bike in the streets.
They told me about the old woman.

My filter, they made the secrets
I learned from them

pure as the water where
the chop of the river lapped sun.

Quarry-edged blocks
of knowledge lodged

in my mind. I did not know.
The buildings were too hard.

The old woman perched
at the top of her house

was its capital.
Cousins flowed round her.

Messages like sails
kept her. She never came downstairs.

She must have smelled
the same bread, watched the ferries.

The stone had loved her
to crumbling.

III

Index, middle and ring
fitted the mountain just across
the river. Across the river
meant, first, a link, wonder.
There, from the kitchen window
to the farms like knuckle-wrinkles,
flat and wide, water. Later,
a separation, wondering at.

. . . spoke of "Melbourne", of "overseas",
I was confused. Where were the castles,
the double-decker buses, the Taj Mahal,
the MCG? Was that Dick Whittington's road
at the base of the mountain? What was beyond?
Apart from the visible connection
with the three-fingertip mountain
I made none. There were
two worlds.

Then Alfred arrived in the street,
seven with an old man's head
and an old man's name. It was wrong.
He was a nazi, a refugee,
dirty, couldn't play cricket.
Alfred, scrubbed and slavic,
and his grandmother with no voice
for English, but dark words
under her shawl linking
the young suburb with unclear
reverberations of old
fears in other places.

Even across the water there was
no Treblinka, Lidice, Hoess.
Later the atlas opened out
one world on a double page.

V

Emblems set high: a bell, a ram's skull,
to force necks into attention, to force
thought. The men who placed them there knew
the first law of propaganda: commitment
follows the expenditure of effort.

The bell, carved in relief from stone
above a shop-front: *Thos Bell & Sons*
was more than a monumental pun.
The original Thos was a convict, Thomas Higg,
brassmonger's lad sent out for stealing a bell.
In 1814 on a gang clearing scrub for a farm
out Lewisham way, and "being troubled by blacks"
he devised a scheme for clearing them as well.

A bell was hung on a pole in a cleared patch.
A few times a day someone would ring it. At dusk
they'd go back the half mile or so to camp.
Soon one bolder native came and tried it,
went back, delighted with the sound, then more
the next night, ringing, laughing at the toy.
The third night the four guards stayed,
bagged three in the dark. From then for years
throughout the area out-parties all took bells.

Freed as reward Higg took up a new name
and after some industrious years' employ
saved enough to set up in business,
his life's token as shop sign to prosper under.
140 years on, the school books
have him as hero. His great great
grandson changed his name to Smith.

The skull, on the other hand, was placed
on the crossbar of a hydro pole
by linesmen, a trophy from
a rather more subtle conflict.

This is "sheep country", pockets of plain
and gorsed escarpments, high to wind
snow and sun. Dumb mutton
turns its harsh elements to fleece
and blown dags. The stupid ram
tups and butts, dies in drought
or spring snow. Animal without
country or cunning, the blind invader
suffers victory, adapts defeat.

This was wallaby country. English grass
has superfined it. Pence a pound
is the measure of colonial success.
The chinless grazier humps the old Merc to town;
Bradford and Osaka nod; their argonauts
return. Everyone's happy. The thaw
runs off to nothing. New growth
browns again under a galvanised sky.

So the skull nailed up says
like a shilling against the sun
"This is man country. Fuck ewe."

Every summer we would drive
through the Midlands, leaving the old port
to stew in its stone. Insulated
from the hills of crows we would speed
through country yellow as a road map
to the coast. Devonport, grandfather's pub
was a haven from history. Whoever made

this town did not believe in emblems,
nailed nothing to lintels. Buildings
themselves embodied the spirit of the time:
1912, built for a future
of peace, dead before the paint
could enter history too. Surface
town, coastal, facing the future
with a blank sea gaze; perfect
facades to hide behind for a holiday
of death, geometrically ornate,
this was as good a place as any
to claim the shallowest family roots.

Interlude

By the Greystone bed, mock-cowboy hat in hand,
shuffling a homage to the poet, to the poetry,
the trapeze artist acknowledges his sawdust base.
Blind eyes and rhinestones meet, the skyway shoots
with song that will not rot, galactic pulse
the twirling hat, the whirling dust combine to will.

> *All day they pump me with paralysis and pain.*
> *They have taken the coursing from my voice, the limp*
> *and stuttering blood is pricked with weird additives.*
> *Curlylocks, Curlylocks, wilt thou be mine?*
> *Mine like the harvest, twisted by bitter wind*
> *out of the blight, hot sweat composting battered roots*
> *spiked with grit, wormed with words, ours, song!*
> *Zither-man, slimmer-man, nor yet feed the swine.*

Yours were the lessons, silent teacher, crafty singer.
Along ten thousand years I learnt by heart in the dark
glory road signposts, learnt to write the hurricanes,
to read the cards, and when I fly from this, our first
meeting, it will be in a machine made by your wit, your work.
I can't make prose to you but I will live our song.

XVI

The stage is the world.
He trissed in lilac, flourishing
a Mannlicher-Carcano 91/38,
hideous to the pit, but from the gods
lisping grace against the pseudo-
Beardsley backdrop. This is style:
derivative from decadence, treading
a step beyond tatty death, turning
entropy on its head. Art has survived
art-for-art's-sake, flaunts its victory
for the sake of art: a performance.

The boy in the lighting box
is on his second bottle of vodka.
The spot wanders. The background changes
slowly from pastels through fiery orange
until its red is insistent, out of proportion
to the language of the play. As for the shot
(or shots), reports conflict. The audience,
questioned in the foyer, was unanimous:
the actor's lips were fuller than is healthy
as if they carried too much blood.
His face otherwise was a cadaver's.
Was this just a matter of make-up?
Those who knew him offstage gave differing answers.
He had disappeared at the instant of blackout.

The victim's brunette widow, meanwhile,
wears his blood becomingly for the TV cameras.
The Secret Service men are grimly handsome.

from *Red Dirt* (1990)

from Red Dirt I

Low Tide, North Esk

"Teach your children well."
— Graham Nash

Yeah, it was simple then. You 'got your shit
together', split from bad scenes and saved the world
by growing your own (dope, hair or vegies),
teaching, trout-fishing. The future was a river.

Cross the Charles Street bridge today. Look down.
Who's getting whose together now? Who's getting split?
No more pentagrams. No more I Ching.
The kids we taught then are all unemployed
again, like '29. Decades of mud
slope into Invermay.

                Up on Barrow
the bald and glittering rocks like skulls and knees
in the Ukraine, sliced by spades of frost
(Well, genocide . . . there's something we know about.)
clarify our beginnings. Sharp and white
the crystal cuts itself to whorls, breaks, grows,
comes down past abattoirs and English willows.

The swamp squeezed down by capital, the weight
of floods and memories of floods, still throws
up the odd swamp fox, that silver greyhound, hope,
lair, cadre, single mum, full-forward.
Under the fog, the simple river slides
round the silos to where our ship comes in.

Macquarie House

"And the lord commended the unjust steward"
— Luke 16:8

You are what you preserve. Generations
of CWA Vacola greengages testify:
a warehouse on every shelf to defy nature,
to soften stone-grey winters, to disburse
everyday exotica at the cold tail-end of a meal.

At the cold tail-end of an empire
household virtues thrived. Accounts were kept.
Narrow, barred windows guarded commodities
stored and recorded like convicts. Set here square
between the bleak plains and the trading ships,

the entrepot has now become a shrine
not to the husbandry of flocks, not to the shearing,
but to the fleecing, to the false manifest
and not the cargo, to the saving of skins.
The town's foundations, theft and thrift, survive.

Today they label history, lock it up
and dole it out. The surplus value
slips through the fog where the estuary
waits, long as a leech. Inventories,
waybills, receipts are shuffled with legerdemain.

This is a town for stewards and accountants:
Room at the top, over the top and away.
Suck what you can. Fatten and fall softly.
The plums plop syrupy from the jar. There's plenty
more where that came from, and as sweet.

Brady's Lookout

"La propriété c'est le vol"
— Proudhon

It is a romance that gallant Matt stood here,
a fiction (not a fantasy; that awaits you
over the hill in weirdest Grindelwald).
Logic and history place him further south,
where the smell of wet sheep and capital still hangs
over the Hobart road,
where the burger and souvenir shops are as tacky
as those bark "inns": the *Royal Oak*
where Matt posted his reward for Arthur's head
and the Woolpack where he coated the door with Kenton's.

And where are they now, the Gunns, the Taylors,
Effingham Lawrences?
And where are all the clowns of Arthur's circus
got up like ringmasters, red targets in the bush?
Still where they were. Only the costumes change.
The power remains. The Western Tiers
are no Sierra Maestra, not even 'romantic scenery'.

This is 'romantic scenery': 'Windermere',
as if it were a lake, not a poisoned river
—another fiction, another romance—:
a cutesie church, an olde worlde pub,
the bourgeoisie playing at being sailors.
But it's a good place to keep a lookout for
what is constant, history that survives.
The coaches still bring people to be robbed.
Lies and betrayal are still our true estate.
The pretty prison keeps us in.

The ladies made a cornucopia of Matt's cell
because he never raped and only killed
redcoats and turncoats. He was so fastidious
he baulked at sharing a coach and gibbet with
Jeffries, who was sick enough to spill a baby's brains against a
gumtree,
who raped people and then ate them.
But even he was not a revolutionary,
just a progenitor of mainstream Tassie culture,
as Matt was of its politics:
making a virtue of impotence,
conning posterity with a flash image.
What hope for an island when even its bushrangers
had no solidarity?

I'll stand here by the tourist coach,
just another wimp who quotes Proudhon
and laments that guerrilla bands have been
romanticised to impotence again.

Reds

for S.P.H

Autumn again: our hopes are melting down.
The weather turns Orcadian. You paint
in wind and watercolours, tidal forms,
the art of exile. This has always been
an island of artists-not-quite-in-residence.
Teachers are exiles. Our message bobs across
a sea to fellow-humans who resist,
know us as alien, cannot trust our fierce
enthusiasms. Old affirmatives,
cheerful as leaves, no stronger, fall, still bright.

Our colleague's dying where the hospital
looks out on rusty trees and murrey rain.
That culture's dying, too, 's a rumour we've
dismissed for decades. Our class enemies,
authoritative as surgeons, just can't wait
to excise vigorous tissue. Only, now,
April and May, I feel their victory,
who have been both doctors and disease.
This is the season for being patient while
malignant cells are breeding at the core.

But let's apply old remedies, fight the flames
of burning books with scarlet fire brigades,
rage red against the danger signs. Our health
is stronger than self-pity. We must build.
A century of scientific love
built Chernobyl. The cancer spreads. What next?

Surely some random active particle
will lodge where it can work a rational,
materialist miracle. After winter, spring.
Artists were always mutants. Working class
kids will baulk at Kulchur, will create
their own responses. Love and hope lie deep.
A sixteen-year-old I'd almost given up on
writes a superb poem - on suicide.

Songs of the Protest Era

(title of an LP advertised on television)

That would have been somewhere
between the Twist and the Frug.
You know, there are people today
who can still do the Twist,
even the Charleston, but it's a pity
that Arthur Murray's black
silhouetted soles never set out
clear instructions for the Protest
or the Frug.

The Napalm was popular then, too.
Nixon sold better than Chubby Checker
— records *and* tapes — and do you remember
that dance we used to do to something by
Creighton Abrams, "They're playing Song My"?
The melody escapes me but the beat's still there
and the steps would soon come back, but I'm not so sure
about those zany dance crazes that swept the campuses
like Kent State.

from White Diamond Gloom

Fluid

A lung full of ice
will stake you out.
The lucid blue
stalactites
drip through.

Who are they who impend?
What qualifications have they
put behind brilliant glass
flat on white rectangular walls?
Where? How tall are they?

You don't want answers, y'know.
The questions hover softly
and will not stab yet.
"Nurse, is this tube
genuine plastic?"

Blade

The first hint is a gleam.
The shell of a wave could be
flattening its curl under the moon.
Then the easy slide

surprises, testing for texture,
finding it smooth, barely
noticeable till the twist
that opens. A tendon gives.

When you clean fish well
a bundle of various organs,
orange, cream, cherry-black,
falls, still compact, out.

from Red Dirt II

Grammar

The runes and ratchets of our time
picked from the soft stone, ore
forged and formed, cog and rhyme,
base and superstructure for
the shape in which we change and grow.
Architecture: history
frozen in the *logos*, so
is language the struggle to be free.

The way men work, the relationship
between them and what they do
shapes the syntax of the age.
As the machines stick and slip,
as the suffixes accrue,
so the lines run on the page.

Song for Seychelles

I

The waves slide in onto the lee shore
gently as the drift of continents.

When the granitic plates sailed off
carrying as trophies Africa and Asia
the stiff backbone of Mahé refused, remained,
until the charming princes of the West
raped her awake, pampered her with vanilla,
cinnamon, mangos, tea, TV and taxis.

II Vallée de Mai

But through the aeons of the lonely coma
monsoons persistently brought dreams of Eden.
Before the cayman grew its legs and died
this was the garden where the deal was made:
the coco-de-mer, the woman's haunch, for life
in paradise: a fair exchange, considering
that jets now fly them back, day-tripping,
making up for lost time. It's now
400 Rupees each for the fruit of knowledge;
a boy will stamp them "paid for" at the gate.
They'd rather look for shells than good or evil.
So Eve in a string bikini squeals at crabs
while Adam hacks at a coconut. Lilith
disguised as a green lizard watches, smiles.
She's seen through the coffin lid, the snorkeller's mask,
been through the glass to wonderland and back.
She knows the pretty past and her old patience
taught her then only to love the future.

III Liberation

Fifth of June, 1977:
a line of surf slices between the red
of coral and the green of takamaka
to make a flag that cuts, shines and continues.

Coconut palms thrown at the sky like starfish
announce the sudden sunrise and embellish
its proclamation. Liberty and justice
are heavy words. Pirates and colonists
threw them overboard, ran light for home.
But the reef held them captive; the sun hit
through the pale shallows; they were there for the taking.
Ashore they stand like the rock at L'Union.

The last bearded corsair's in port in Europe;
he's left his doubloons buried in the sky.
Pieces of sweat glint, fish-scales in the sun.
That will be capital enough to build
a miracle. Where fish and foxes fly
ideals can leap into reality.

from *The Streets Aren't for Dreamers* (1995)

Stage Dive

Not always living by proxy, nor re-living
the clip of edited glamour thrash,
the fantasy death gig safe as the States,
no, sometimes, having so heavy a need to fly
on a lead break of my own, to assert
more than dreary frenzy can: noise pure beyond sound,
a tattoo sharper than art or pain,
I make and am still and private.

Anyone can jump from the top of an amp
into a crowd. Faith in the music, in the stance,
is a bungy rope. You might as well
sit in the mall or round a bong.
You might as well mutter, "The world's fucked"
to your mates who know that's not news.

"Despair" is no more to the point
than "the devil." When the metal
gets to be more than metaphor
it's style driven all the way
till it fuses with reality.

Like when Jason's head banged back
that night we were just having a few beers
no smart-arse video director
put the clotted pink crap
on my Anthrax T-shirt.

Now I mime to the tape of his suicide
but with feeling; the memory of his sudden weight

in my arms is the bass line to a track
I'll cut one day. When I dive
it will be through all this shit and on forever.

Words for K

So now he rapes my brain by saying 'sorry'
and I bury my hair in cold sand,
swim naked in the winter ocean,
climb high to hell's ice.

Sixteen years of Daddy
bursting through clouds of brimstone dust
from the family bible, the chapel organ pumping
at my blood, at my baby innards, Mum's eyes
like vicious prayers, the circle closed
as a country congregation.

I was seventeen
when I first dared look in a mirror.
I still sleep on my stomach
in case Satan through the floorboard cracks
takes me by surprise again
to make me his favourite daughter.

And folders, drawers, rooms, mountains
won't hold all my words, my formulae,
my poems. There's no climate
the sane and faithful live in
that my statistics can describe.

Hold me but don't touch me.

*Cardia Lola**: Arramaieda at the Oak

Out of tune only with the times,
the a cappella voices rise
defiant as the *lola* Walyer stole
and taught her sisters to use
against the 'ghosts' in 1828.
"I have been with the ghosts
and they have not held me,"
she told her men at Panatana.

Sold to the sealers for dogs and flour,
Walyer, like the singers' namesake, fought
when men gave up or died, when other women
sang hymns with Robinson in floral frocks.
Out of tune with greed and apathy,
her *lola* sang with a pure pitch
that shatters still. "They have not held me."

Here in this pub the ghosts of ghosts
drink with today's sealers, sleaze and grope
— no dogs, no flour, perhaps a bottle
of sweet, cheap wine — but not tonight.
Tonight the discipline of harmony
will liberate, a magic equal to
Walyer's *cardialola* against one
of the two things she taught us to fear and hate:
a white man and a black snake.

Cardialola: 'several guns' in the Western Pallawah language

Arriving in Devonport

Driving into a smashed-bottle sunset,
tape-deck spilling k d like blood and honey
into a pit, I know just how the next town waits.

Oil tanks patrol the river bank where the bridge reaches,
tentative, into the back-lit heart, a syringe of hope.
I'm sliding with the music through the streets.

I know the pubs will smell of guns, divorce,
dealerships and bigotry: too flat, too shallow
for any despair deeper than talk-back summons.

No matter how smartly plate-glass fashion slices
the hum of truth from the drum of lust for distance
hope doesn't empty showrooms or fill freezer-packs.

This town knows that. I park, cut the music
with the motor. In the river local wisdom slaps
the hull of the ferry to the anxious world.

Bear

When they put that play on
down at the community centre
I was a bear. I scared the first three rows
of welfare workers silly.

Mostly when I roar it's not an act,
more of a drama. The worst thing
is not being able to tell them,
clearly, to shut up.

Not drunk, not stupid, only
angry: I won't get in that bus
with SPASTIC painted on it:
I am grizzly with pride,

polar with disdain. In the street
I lumber, shamble, but in
the straight line of the hunt.
I am not cuddly.

from *Thorne's Best Bitter* (2006)

Mesopotamian Suite

1. Ace

In September 2002 the White House Chief of Staff,
Andrew H Card Jr, when asked by reporters
why the US had not yet invaded Iraq,
answered, "From a marketing point of view,
you don't introduce new products in August."

Andy, when the chips, as they say, are down,
I want you in my hand or up my sleeve.
Not even your boss, the joker, for all his bluff
could deal a line as wild as that:
the spin on the spin on the spin.

While we wasted millions of non-combatant words
on pedantic points of morality or strategy,
while we marched or debated, worried or cheered,
you showed a sensitivity in tune with the turning year
like a nature poet or General Motors executive.

Some of us never learn. My last book was launched
in August. It didn't sell anywhere near as well
as *Shock and Awe* nor did it sever as many limbs.
Perhaps if I piled the critics in a naked pyramid...
But then that August thing,
it's for the Northern Hemisphere, right?

2. Fallujah Face-off, April 2004

Scared teenagers steal hubcaps
off the war machine and know
only religion and danger.
There hasn't been time to learn
the history of last year's war,
let alone of this year's peace.
They cannot trust their officers
but they can be sure of Allah and of pain.

Across the two-lane blacktop
Justin Timberlake and Britney Spears
stand wide-eyed in battle fatigues
on a flat desert page from an atlas
they never opened. The flag and the music
provide the substance of their faith.
Their weapons are heavy but they get
regular e-mails from their pastors.

Alongside the road runs a pipeline
full of thick, black democracy
at $40 a barrel. It is oblivious,
having been dead for millions of years.

3. Two Purty Gals from West Virginia

Jessica, we all pentagonised
over your fate; we heard about
the stab wounds and the rape,
the evil doctors and the rescue
with cameras blazing. And now
we sympathise with your amnesia.
Children adorn your internet shrines
with bad poems. There is no doubt
that you are the most photogenic Pfc
ever to be lied about for a bad cause.

Lynndie, we can forgive
the pointing finger, the leash, the cheeky grin,
but not the spelling of your name.
You were only following orders.
They weren't even Americans.
But what were your parents thinking?

4. Shake 'n' Bake

"Gingerbread White House: View of the North Portico, 100 pounds (34 sheets) of gingerbread, 150 pounds of white and dark chocolate, Clear, poured sugar windows, One strand of white lights inside the Gingerbread White House make it glow." — White House Press Release, Christmas 2005

Make it glow. Make it glow. Make it glow.
White phosphorus over Fallujah, a hundred times sheet lightning:
the *illuminati* stagger out,
ripping away clothes, skin.
What were handfuls of flesh pour between fingers.
Breathing fluid fire, the too-bright smell,
they are not dead. Thirty seconds, forty-five,
then the high explosive follow-up
and all their Christmasses come at once,
as the saying goes.

Every child knows about the witch in the gingerbread house,
about the glow from ovens.
Jenna and Barb jr are too grown-up
to play "knock-knock" at the sugar panes, to dare each other.
Fairy tales belong to the land
of faraway, of Scheherazade, saved by stories,
whose statue in Iraq has not been toppled.
Her saying goes and goes. She goes, "Onceuponatime . . ."
There was a city. A strand of white lights
made it glow.

5. The Code of Hammurabi

The Code of Hammurabi, once king of these parts, says:
"If anyone bring an accusation of any crime before the elders,
and does not prove what he has charged,
he shall, if it be a capital offence charged,
be put to death." When in Mesopotamia
do as the Mesopotamians do.
GWB. WMD. QED.

6. Baghdad Bazaar

What's on special today? Human life is still going cheap.
You can get Democracy in a special cut-rate package.
The voting bit has been taken out because the customers
would never get the hang of how to use it.

Sovereignty's a giveaway. Part of the label's come off
but if you look hard you can read the bit that says,
". . . as long as you do what you're told."
What's that? No, we don't stock Reconciliation.

You could buy a used flying carpet from Chalabi.
The clock's only been wound back to 1978
and it's very light on gas, which is just as well
as we don't actually own any these days.

What do you mean you'll shop around?
We already have your credit card details
in the computer. You can expect a visit.
Now, how about some cheap antiquities?

7. Alabama

"I got my kills, I'm coming down. I just love my job."
— Sergeant James Anyett, US 1st Infantry, Fallujah, 2004

Last year it was whitetail in Barbour County,
the smell of pines and blood sweet as youth.
Daddy got my first kill mounted
as a 21st birthday present.
When my three littl'uns grow up
I'll take them to where the breeze off Lake Eufaula
makes you glad to be an Alabamian
and teach them manhood, teach them
about the subtle differences between
Remingtons and Winchesters.

There are no longleaf pines here, no yellowhammers,
but I've got my buddies; I've got better gear
than back home even and I'm being paid.
Bagged five this morning. Goddam shame
they won't let you take them home as trophies.
Although a couple were undersize and one was pregnant,
but those're just as hard to hit as the big buck towelheads.
They were going to bring in mortars, but I said:
Dude, give me the sniper rifle. I can take them out.
I'm from Alabama.

8. Purrfect Angelz

"Our performers are highly trained with years of experience and a positive attitude."
— Purrfect Angelz website

They went down well at the Full Throttle Biker Rally.
Now they're in Baghdad for the boys.
They sing. They dance. They acrobatise.
They wear . . . well, not much really,
but the hotpants are in regulation army colours.

Dayna, Deena, Monet and Shay Lyn
are spreading for the delectation of the troops
the values of the homeland, arousing
morale, reminding us of all the metaphors
of war and lust, and of a woman's place.
Re-energised after the show,
our highly trained personnel
go back to Abu Ghraib and put
their years of experience to work,
displaying a positive attitude.

9. And the Poets Fled

*"And the poets fled, no longer able to think
or sing in the midst of the horror."*
— Tariq Ali

The cuneiform entries in Sumerian accounts
are still bleeding, wedges cut into the clay we are all made from,
notches keeping the score of harm and hope
from Ur to Halliburton's laptop screens
while history is written by arm-stumps in the sand
and rolls along the bottom of the CNN newscasts.

Where is the library of Sennacherib?
And who can read its books now?
And whatever happened to the Baghdad Poetry Festival?
The questions must assail the Green Zone like car bombs,
as insistent as the bare-handed crowds
who ripped collaborators apart in '58.

The poet Saadi Youssef wrote "The Jackals' Wedding"
from exile, sent it through cyberspace
faster than a Sidewinder and more deadly
to those who would never have sat at the jackals' wedding feast
whether it was the Medes or the Janissaries
or Negroponte who gave the bride away.

The poets will return. Saadi Youssef
will return as his poems already have.
Mudhaffar al-Nawab will return, and Sinan Antoon.
In the wine bars of Abu-Nuwwas Street we shall hear again
cluster-poems explode, watch heat-seeking poems
find their targets in the hearts and brains of friends.

Dentist's Waiting Room

Flicking through the mags checking the tsunami diet,
the asylum seeker's boob job and Terri Schiavo's horoscope,
I asked myself, "If Camilla can become Princess of Wales,
why can't Shane Warne be the next Pope?"
It would, of course, be more in keeping with tradition
if those roles were reversed, but let's not think too deeply
about such weighty matters; let's instead
amuse our winter selves with poolside skimming
through the glossy travel supplement of *Island*
imagining those cute poems with little umbrellas over them.
When *Ten Days of Ten Eighty* comes along I know it's time
to head for the intellectual stimulus of Port Douglas.
Pass the history wars brand sunblock and my
Reconciliation sarong, the green one.

But before I go, a quick cap and polish;
when I smile, wide as a thylacine, I want
to be described as photogenic.

Villanelles of the New Morality

I

Shout hallelujah, praise the Lord and sing!
Let Jesus in your life to make you rich.
'God is love' no longer means a thing.

Each day we let our fervent prayers take wing:
"Dear Lord, please scratch our aspirational itch."
Shout hallelujah, praise the Lord and sing!

The more you pray, the more your prayers bring
DVDs, plasma screens and other kitsch.
'God is love' no longer means a thing.

Poverty's sinful and embarrassing.
Christ will raise you from that fetid ditch.
Shout hallelujah, praise the Lord and sing!

Hold fast to your faith and be unwavering
so that your path to wealth will know no hitch.
'God is love' no longer means a thing

and the word 'peace' has an atheistic ring.
Buy shares in a bank; it doesn't matter which.
Shout hallelujah, praise the Lord and sing!
'God is love' no longer means a thing.

II

'Whatever it takes' is now the way to go.
A batsman who walks earns his teammates' contempt.
Sportsmanship is weakness. This we know.

Whatever the game, whether amateur or pro,
only success is worthy of the attempt.
'Whatever it takes' is now the way to go.

If it's not seen by ref or video
it didn't happen. As long as dollars tempt,
sportsmanship is weakness. This we know.

Before you run or jump or ride or throw,
consult your lawyers, sleek, well-fed and kempt.
'Whatever it takes' is now the way to go.

In war, too, you must strike the initial blow,
some potential future sortie to pre-empt.
Sportsmanship is weakness. This we know.

In every action we must act as though
from the rules' spirit we hold ourselves exempt
'Whatever it takes' is now the way to go.
Sportsmanship is weakness. This we know.

III

The bombs come down out of the blinding blue.
A hospital stood here and now there's dust.
The end of decency is a beginning, too.

The world's morality is made anew.
Back home the voters exercise bloodlust.
The bombs come down out of the blinding blue.

Compassion's now the ultimate taboo.
Each sniper's gun is stamped "In God We Trust".
The end of decency is a beginning, too.

The faithful rise from every padded pew
and sing with arms and hearts to heaven upthrust.
The bombs come down out of the blinding blue

and children die because the aim is true,
These bombs are blessed. The bombers' cause is just.
The end of decency is a beginning, too.

I helped destroy Fallujah. So did you;
we told our leaders, "Kill them if you must."
The bombs come down out of the blinding blue.
The end of decency is a beginning, too.

from *A Letter to Egon Kisch* (2007)

VIII

A while back there I wrote about the flag
and how some want to change it: others not.
Of late we've seen how every bronzed ratbag
racist beach bum who's feeling insecure
and thinks that wog-bashing's exactly what
he needs to boost his ego, reassure
himself that he is stronger, whiter, bolder's
not armed until it's draped across his shoulders.

All tried and true flags have a soubriquet:
the "Stars and Stripes", the good old "Union Jack".
Australia's come of age because today
(Forget about that 'roo in boxing gloves.)
no longer does our Aussie banner lack
a nickname, one that everybody loves.
The way our Aussie culture's taking shape,
nothing's more apt than the "Cronulla Cape".

It was that Pommie, Churchill, who once said,
"We'll fight them on the beaches . . ." but the Brits
don't have real beaches. It's our sand runs red
with blood (and, I keep forgetting it, the Turks')
The rallying emblem of all racist shits,
surf club neo-Nazis, loser berks,
One Nation airheads and like-minded dross
is that Blue Ensign with its Southern Cross.

There was a time when public sentiment
was all in favour of a change of flag.
Few tears were shed when our old anthem went,
although a lot would have preferred that song

about jumbucks, a swagman and his swag,
and billies boiling by the billabong,
but it was just too downbeat, I suppose.
"Advance Australia Fair" is what we chose.

But that's about as far as we would go.
Suggest a new flag and the old farts go ape.
"It waved above us when we fought the foe,"
the RSL and hangers-on all thunder.
And so we're stuck with the Cronulla Cape.
It flies to show that we shall never sunder
the ties that bind us to the House of Windsor,
whatever hue our politics or skins are.

Ah, there's the rub: the rub of 15+⊠.
We lie around on beaches to get tanned,
but underneath the skin what makes us us
is our essential whiteness. Dinkum Aussies
get their dark skins from lying on the sand
wearing not much except the briefest cossies.
Bronzed and bonzer? You don't qualify,
if it comes naturally. You have to try.

We've politicians who have made an art
of playing that old game of us and them.
You couldn't call them racist; they're too smart
(except for Danna Vale) to let it show.
They can't afford to have the press condemn
them but they know just how to blow
the dog whistle that, thanks to their cunning,
the racist dogs all hear and so come running.

The white man's burden's what the flag's about.
It stood for "Empire!" everywhere it flew
back when no British colony was without

a Union Jack in its flag's canton. Now
it's us, New Zealand, Fiji, Tuvalu;
the rest have made it clear they won't allow
a foreign flag to dominate. We learn
so slowly, if at all. "Burn, baby, burn!"

Changing the flag would give some indication
that the real world is where Australia lives.
At present we're by far the largest nation
that has a foreigner as Head of State.
What's more, it seems that no one really gives
a royal toss. Checked Lizzie's dos of late?
Watched as the invited guests arrive —
among them Aussies, Rolf, Germaine and Clive?

If they're quite happy to endorse the rule
of unelected chinless German bores
then who'd be game enough to ridicule
the antics of the monarchists back here?
Almost as up-to-date as dinosaurs,
they get their politics from *New Idea*.
There's no way a sane person could defend 'em,
but they did win the bloody referendum.

You see, Egon, in 1999
some of us thought it might be time to start
the process of beginning to design
a constitution that allowed a choice
of who our Head of State might be. At heart
(or so we thought) Australians want a voice
in matters such as this; that's democratic.
The rebuff to such ideas was emphatic.

A clear majority gave a loud "No"
to a republic. They would rather cling

like loyal subjects to the status quo.
As our next leader they'd prefer a prince
who'd rather be a tampon than a king.
Not even Malcolm Turnbull could convince
Australians to make that simple change.
The rest of the world now thinks we're very strange.

Royalty has its uses, I'll admit.
The one important fact you can't avoid
is: you can make a quid if you're a Brit
who's selling tourist tat to Yanks. It keeps
photographers and sycophants employed
and publishers of magazines make heaps,
but that doesn't provide much consolation
for those who want to choose who heads this nation.

We are, of course, self-governing. It's not
as if the sovereign made real decisions.
But seeing as that is the case, then what
is wrong with letting everybody know
just how it is? Perhaps the world's derision's
a price to pay that we consider low
enough, 'cause they already mock us
for being uncultured, uncouth, boorish Ockers.

I'd rather be described as lacking couth
than as owing allegiance to that bunch.
You'd have remembered, Egon, in your youth
you knew them as the Saxe-Coburg-Gothas.
In 1917 they had a hunch
that waging war against those German rotters
might have a downside, so in one fell swoop
they were renamed — after a thin brown soup.

Saxe-Coburg-Gotha thus became
Windsor, though George still had a German accent.
You don't change families when you change your name.
World War One was just a family feud
though actual family members stayed well back, sent
young men as proxies till a multitude
of them lay dead and rotting in the mud
of Europe. Well, you can't spill royal blood.

Of course these royal families intermarried,
bred out their chins and wits and kept the lines
more or less pure, while many of them carried
on with members of the lower orders,
had byblows born to tarts and concubines.
Flings and affairs weren't thought too untoward as
work was always there for royal pimps an'
they all tried to forget that Wallis Simpson.

Everyone loves a bit of juicy slander
about the rich. The Windsors are fair game,
like film and sport stars. Magazines will pander
to our desires to bring them down a peg
or two. Envying their wealth and fame,
we fantasize about what Princess Meg
got up to on Mustique or whether Hewitt
is Harry's dad, or whether Charles did do it

with some valet or footman. We might say
that we don't care, but Di's death really rocked us.
A bimbo kindy aide who got in way
beyond her depth, she probably deserved
our sympathy. It's certain the spin doctors
needed something after we'd all perved
on pics of Fergie topless, tales of sex an'
luxury, her toes sucked by some Texan.

And what this has to do with us down here
on the planet's underside is that they're still
our royals. We line the streets and cheer
and wave Cronulla Capes and Union Jacks
when Mrs Windsor visits, and the bill
is covered out of what we pay in tax.
And now, thanks to the referendum's failure,
until she dies she'll be Queen of Australia.

XII

You wrote at length about the situation
of those Australians who'd got here first.
Murder by arsenic at Kilcoy Station,
rape of Kungarri girls, Arthur's Black Line:
the past, you knew,'d been bad, but far the worst
was that the present era showed no sign
that things were better. Down at La Perouse
you saw kids peddling more than didgeridoos.

You wrote of Hughie Noble who had fought
in World War One and for South Sydney, too,
reduced to showing tricks to tourists. Sport,
no less than courage under fire, had failed
to lift him. Like the boomerangs he threw,
Hughie kept coming back to what was hailed
as "living culture", playing his grotesque
role as exemplar of the "picturesque".

Nowadays we're not so patronising,
or so we'd like to think. Whitefellas pay
big bucks for desert art. It's not surprising
that there are lots of rich white dealers whom
we can thank because at last today

all races can contribute to the boom
in art. Old Hughie would have nodded; he
knew firsthand of culture as commodity.

On boardroom walls there's work whose makers squat
in dust and flies while battling diabetes.
Their paintings go for fifty bucks per dot
at least (that's retail), but the artist's share
(So much for reconciliation, treaties
compacts and so on!) is never anywhere
near what the dealers rake in. Well, so what?
Isn't poverty the artist's lot?

It's like this, Egon. Whilst we used to be
a philistine, uncultured mob in Oz,
now we've got tickets on ourselves, you see.
There are some suburbs where it's quite OK
to be an artist. Unlike how it was
when you were here, Australians will pay
enough so that some artists do all right,
but those that do all happen to be white.

It's only slightly better, mate, in sport.
When Hughie ran round for the Rabbitohs
the fans' his teammates' and the club's support
stopped at the gates. Racist taunts were part
of how the game was played and I suppose
they still are in some places but a start
was made in AFL when Nicky Win-
mar pulled up his jumper, pointed to his skin

and said, "So what?" (or words to that effect).
Since then in Aussie Rules if you're heard callin'
a player a black cunt you can expect
a fine or a suspension — though you get

no penalty of any kind at all in
cases where you drop the epithet.
Sexism's not regarded as a crime.
We tend to take one issue at a time.

I guess the height of Koori sporting pride
was Cathy winning gold, though there were those
who said of that, "They should be satisfied
now; surely they don't want land rights as well."
Of course for each indigenous kid who grows
up to win medals or play AFL
there's hundreds die too young, or try to cope
by drinking, sniffing petrol, blowing dope.

Whitefellas sit and watch and say it's not
their fault. They didn't steal the land. The blame
goes back too many generations. "What
do previous policies, however cruel,
have to do with us today?" This lame
approach echoes what I was taught in school:
Tasmanian Aborigines are gone,
wiped out, extinct as the diprotodon.

And so, sad though it be, we own their lands
but cannot give them back. It's far too late.
So let's all buy the soap to wash our hands
where Pontius Pilate bought his. "Love means
never having to say you're sorry." Hate
means never wanting to. What's most obscene's
the fact that while we fight about who's lying
a culture's being trashed and kids are dying.

from *Yeah No* (2012)

La Cave d'Aristide

It is not the world which passes our long-legged, small table
outside the Cave d'Aristide where we have hoisted ourselves
to settle on the slightly too-high stools.

With my dark glasses and light air,
my T-shirt striped horizontally, the image I am striving for
is more *faux Francais* than *vrai Palavasien*.

Irony! Somehow this village condones its ease.
No, it's not 'the world', certainly not as literal
translation, but it's more than fellow-tourists,

who are few despite the excellence
of the picpoul de pinet, the beach, the sunlight,
the exchange rate and the mussels.

This spot, right on the corner
of Rue Aristide Briand,
is perfect for remembering his victims:

Paul Boible, railway worker, before the court
in 1910 for carrying a prohibited weapon,
to wit a corkscrew, the thousands

who tore up their mobilisation orders
and mailed the scraps to Aristide, the Pais sparks
done out of their jobs by soldiers.

Ah, Aristide, it was Emma Goldman
who countered your scream of 'sabotage' with,
'Who but the most ordinary philistine will call that a crime?'

If there was a wine bar on some Rue Emma Goldman
somewhere, I'd be drinking there with the *cheminots*,
and Paul Boible would pull my cork.

But for now it's Aristide, and the sun sets
as the shopkeepers' kids play in the street
and I turn to my Mas Daumas Gassac '06

and ask myself how ordinary a philistine I am.
Aristide, you were the prototype
for Chifley, Blair and the Social Democrats

who (let's be kind) spun themselves into
contradiction. Were you, were any of them
aware of this? Here, on my stool,

(no armchair Marxist!) I can contemplate
not just the passing 'life', not just the wine,
but how my hedonism and my history

have put me here, my feet just off the pavement,
glad of not having to strike for five francs a day
and with the luxury of pretending to pretension.

Write the Future

for the Greek workers May 2010

Cristiano Ronaldo
has replayed Jonnie Walker
on the giant billboard
across from the ferry wharf,
but he is neither running
nor kicking, let alone striding.
When all you have to sell
is your self, no matter
for how many millions
how much are you human?

"Write the future" the slogan:
the swoosh is a carelessly
flicked mark of ownership.
Here, now, in Piraeus
the future has been written
with keystrokes quicker than
Cristiano's Nike'd feet
(which stand planted, as is
even the highest paid striker
can stop work) by dead money's
dead hand.

Gnomic

All you need is an Ern Malley garden gnome
and the world's your ostrich, or something.
Last time I strolled the promenades of Portoroz
most of the other millionaires were on rollerblades.
Now *that* is post-imperialism for you.
But I can't handle anything more complex
than issues of mere style; hence the question
of garden mini-statuary. There is a factory
on the outskirts of Shanghai where
small plaster likenesses of the great hoax poet
are produced cheaply, along with those of
Ben Cousins (complete with 'Such is Life' tattoo),
that Spencer girl who married above her station
and died in a tunnel, Neil Bush and various other
members of the celebrity tribe.

Post-imperialism meets post-Disney
and it 'never ceases to amaze' me
that there are some people who still prefer
Hippy, Sleazy, Basho and whatever else
the Magnificent Seven were called,
or who are so insensitive
to inter-species issues that they pose their gnomes
by ponds with fishing rods. I mean, really,
would you pose one with a gun or a noose?
Perhaps one dressed as an Austro-Hungarian officer,
with sabre discreetly sheathed, as if
promenading in Portoroz in the good old days.

Gallarta

i.m. Larry Knight, died underground, Beaconsfield, Tasmania 25 April 2006

On the edge of the open cut
which used to be a city
young men, stripped in the iron sun,
hurl crowbars down at blocks
or rock, laughing at each others' muscles.
On the surface competition —
cycling, pelota, *futbol* —
work as pure fun.

           Underground
co-operation means life.

The young woman in the mining museum
explains to my broken Spanish
how they pulled down Gallarta
and rebuilt it over there.
When I ask about the house
where La Pasionaria was born
her smile is seismic.

           In mining towns
they know what really matters.

Suburban Subversion

Someone should have told the wattlebirds
that Malcolm McLaren has died,
that Sid is well dead and Nancy
is murdered again and again
with every Google search.
But no-one has, and their calls
stab, extra-large safety pins
puncturing the grevilleas' tartan.

Smoother and reassuring
the leaf blower is a symphony
of earnest joy, as if Beethoven
were orchestrating the
transformation of diesel, through
kinetic energy, to tidiness,
a triumph after long, smart wars.
Control lulls, soothes. Nectar disrupts.

Elegy for Shelton

Shelton, I got the better deal:
adopted out of a rich Toorak family
instead of into one. Our Welsh mothers,
our blood family, both loved poetry.
Mine, as she lay dying, asked for Dylan Thomas.
Yours could have had her own Rimbaud,
but one with elegance, the thieving child
who never outgrew the need to write,
to dazzle, to swing along the chuck-clotted lanes
with a cane and a gold-topped stanza,
keeping that angel face towards the world, towards
the next reading, the next hit,
the next sweet man or woman.

That last night when you were slipping
into the blue smoke cloud of no more,
we were both strong: no recanting,
no regrets (it was easier for me). We vowed
solidarity and it wasn't just the lines
written by chance, recited by flamboyant
coincidence, that tied us together.
Those lines and our own, performed,
cast to charm, pressed in books
like perverse flowers, now hang loose,
but I still hold on.

Little Pataphysics (2021)

He's my blonde-headed stompie-wompie real gone surfer boy.
Joe Halford and Jay Justin

Cliches are the armature of the Absolute.
Alfred Jarry

Little Patronage

The cast of *Ubu Roi* weren't in it for
the toxic sugar of applause
but what 14-year-old could resist sweets?
The breakers of fame were another matter;

they called for a skill to ride them safely,
each curled frill a threat so that
nerve had to be held as well as balance,
but Pattie sang because she loved to.

Imagine 'Pataphysical Drama on Netflix'
or Disney buying the rights to the Absurd.
But then, what if a blonde teenager
had stomped into a Jarry play and owned it?

Little Patchwork

They would have looked from the old-fangled
flying machine to Alfred had he
ascended like a cobbled quilt:
the farms of France. The beaches of Sydney,

more like tender blankets, curled
around the living spaces of people
who were shockable but no less real
than those who stomped their applause

in Paris or Coogee, squaring
the weird light into portions,
frenzied with laughter or just
swallowing the rhythm again and again.

Little Patagonia

Faustroll and Panmuphle surfed over Paris
the way Johnny and Pattie danced
all over the sand. At the end
neither pair could find their monkey.

The wilderness of South America
with its Gondwanan flora
could be said to be 'Pushing a Good Thing
Too Far'. So forget geobiology

and just 'Dance, Puppet, Dance'.
Ah, those songs of the mindless days!
And those plays of the mindless throngs!
The tectonic plates have moved on.

Little Patch

A small dog yapping and nipping as if
bred to irritate the bourgeoisie:
not to upset anyone too much,
more like a play that didn't make 'sense',

Patch ran along the beach scaring waves,
not worrying the seagulls. Alfred
sat among the fashionable crowd
who smiled enigmatically

at each line they didn't understand.
Pattie just sang and smiled as if
she was having fun with no burden,
philosophical, theatrical or otherwise.

Little Patriarch

Alfred didn't live long enough
to become a patriarch
but he is still the grandfather
of the absurd.

Pattie won against the patriarchy
but will be eternally fourteen
and stomping away in the cause of
having innocent fun.

Some of us try to make our lives
a combination of theirs.
We aspire to mock *gravitas*
but keep the sand between our toes.

Little Patefaction

When the curtain went up on another
performance of *Ubu Roi* or when
Pattie came on stage, or whenever
the 'show' opened, there was a thrill

expecting what? Perfection yet again?
Or not expecting, keeping the brain blank
of hope: an empty screen, an opened
notebook, waiting for the intro riff.

Just as the boy out on the furthest break
waits for the sea to rise and throw him forward,
so in the back row of the theatre
Jarry's audience were eagerly empty.

Little Patchouli

and sea-grass matting, flowing hair and
dresses, less than a decade after
Pattie's acme, listening to ...
Donovan? in a positive haze

was our entry to the holy nonsense.
The 'science of imaginary solutions'
grew from our grandparents' time
but in between was a sad, tough generation

of Two-World-Wars-and-a-Depression,
stinking of parental concerns,
tough love and crooners, logic
and satisfying plot lines.

Little Paterson

I came down from the outback,
a dry and dusty land,
and here I am at Bronte
close by the golden sand.

There's this here bloke in Paris
who wrote some crazy play
but even he would find it hard
describing this display.

This blonde-haired teenage kiddie
is belting out a song.
There's rhythm but no melody,
but, hey, I'll sing along.

Little Patible

It is the shorter arm, the transom
of the Cross, the one to which
the wrists are tied, not nailed,
which bears the weight

like a surfboard. Someone wrote
that the serious critics crucified
Pattie when the 45 single
of 'He's My Blonde-' etc came out,

but the sales rolled in like breakers
from Malibu across the ocean
to Bronte, Coogee and Maroubra
and we rode them to Easter and beyond.

Little Patella

When a kneecap cracks
the pain stabs two ways.
Ankle and hip take it,
arc to the brain and back

The world is not solid.
It is negotiated softly,
without sufficient panic
by politicians or lovers.

Inside the tube no sky
can shelter, no sand
can soothe. The vacuum
is made of speed.

Little Patisserie

With what sweet treats shall we woo
the Little Aussie Stomper?
Almond croissants and chocolate éclairs,
petits fours like jewels on a tray.

The tributes we lay before Ubu Roi
are grimmer: curled bodies of babies killed
by plague or hunger. Tyranny knows
neither pastry nor blonde icing.

Escoffier and Jarry grew up together.
They had different ideas about
fantasy but both of them understood
the charm of the simple beat.

Little Patrician

Malcolm Turnbull and the Amphlett family
all come from the right side of town
(if you stand in Hyde Park facing North)
but Mal never stomped

at a Bronte Surf Club gig
while the now Mrs P. Thelma Thompson
fronted the Statesmen
with Duncan McGuire on bass.

Statesmen? There was that phone call
with Trump, who wished he'd been in the front row
for cousin Chrissy's famous flash,
but she was from Geelong, so ...

Little Patrick White

Across the mystic red-roofed East,
Moore Park to Maroubra,
where Manoly in a blonde wig
hangs ten, the heroic tanned Aussie,

and long-haired muses sun themselves,
inspiring lotioned sleaze or art,
while others drink in darkened public bars
wiped clean of last night's music,

teenagers smack the bases
of sauce bottles so deftly
that the black crust is avoided
as the red reality flows.

Little Patriotism

I remember when Anzac Day only meant
drunks in the small town gutters.
We didn't visit my ex-RAAF uncles
or listen to small politicians

who promoted themselves with clichés
and badges. I can only imagine
the Maroubra RSL in those days
before Pattie was born.

Ubu has always been my liege.
Loyalty to his disreputable
absurdity the oath taken on a turd.
Flags flag, as intended, surely.

Little Patricide

I have killed my father just as
he killed me. No Père Ubu, he
disposed of my existence. My Mother
disposed of my body to adoption.

As a teenager I sang
not stompie-wompie surf songs
but land-based blues. Now
I have lived a lifetime without him,

but not without regret. My brothers,
despite having more reason,
refrained from killing him. Was it weakness
or ignorance that spurred my crime?

Little Patmos

Halfway up the hill is the cave
where John wrote his Revelation.
You can get ripped off for souvenirs
or you can go back down to the beach.

I stood upon the sand of the sea,
and saw a beast rise up out of the sea,
and it rode a giant wave until it reached
Pattie waiting with a towel and a song.

Ubu was also a surfer and certainly
a beast. Alfred and John between them
had enough imagination
to create even a teen idol.

previously unpublished

The Golden Mile

I used to be that poet bloke,
Tim Thorne, a Burnie boy
adrift along the Golden Mile,
lost in teen bewilderment
and making unremarkable mistakes.

Never had the words in those days
but they were coming slowly,
slower than the hormones
but faster than the accommodation
of death and lesser complaints.

Ah, the Golden Mile, measured now
in metric post-modern empty shops
where more than the food is junk,
it spans my elderly brain
like a line misread from a Beat.

The school was at one end of the Mile,
the undertakers at the other.
The symbolism never occurred to me then
but it seems too obvious now
to be at all believable.

The Beats, anyhow, were more about life
and it was life I was anticipating.
Now I remember how I hoped
to shine like the Golden Mile
back when I was Tim Thorne.

Chemo

Don't use the word "battle". Battles are not
what I do. My uncle was in a battle.
It had a name, "Gallipoli". Absurd and pointless,
just look at a map of the world, Australia
and New Zealand trying to invade Turkey.
Cancer is not the Ottoman Empire.

My post-op ward-mate, Steve, was more of a man
for battles. He would wake me up with his
"Get me my guns! I'm gonna shoot my way out of here!"
until beneath the curtain six pairs of steel-caps marched in
to demonstrate bedside manner. The only guns,
anyway, were on the cops guarding the next ward.

Nor mention "journey". Roberto in the other bed
had made a journey, but not linguistically.
I was the only person on the floor
who had Italian and could understand his screams,
which I would have translated as, "Will someone please
tell me what is going on?" but they had sliced away my voice.

After the op I made a journey,
to Bellingen and Port Macquarie:
Bello for the music and my troubadaughter,
Port Mac for a restaurant named after a Forbes collection,
"The Stunned Mullet", whose scallops come from Canada
where they excise the roe as if it were a tumour.

Then back home where the cancers are on the devils
and metastase across the landscape as plantations
of greed and *nitens*: Tasmania! I would weep for you
but the cytotoxins have turned my tears to poison.

Epitaph

I did not pass. I failed
to stay alive. There is no other side.
Death is not a wall but a void.
I shall have written this in advance:
the only future perfect that there is.

Notes

For My Father: "Seeking heroics, we become absurd" is from "Home Movies", published in Tim's first book, *Tense Mood and Voice*, (Lyre-Bird Writers 1969).

The Aisles: The epigraphic line introduces the song, "The Isles of Greece" in *Don Juan*. "Yet in these times he might have done much worse" is part of Byron's appraisal of the song (which, of course, he wrote himself). Hence the reference to irony. "George" is Byron (but it could, at a paronomasial stretch, be Johnston; the cliffs of Hydra are indeed charmin').

Bronte Country: Doris Leadbetter, a much underrated performance poet, lived in Haworth before migrating to Australia.

Leipzig: This poem starts from an incident in 1989 when demonstrators, fleeing from the police who were under orders from the government to shoot to kill (Honecker was the East German President), sought refuge in the Gewandhaus during a concert under the baton of Kurt Masur. As traditionally was supposed to have happened in churches in earlier times, the police declined to pursue them.

Lockout: John Brown was the manager of the Rothbury mine at the time of the lockout. "Our Norm" was Norm Brown (needless to say, no relation), the only direct fatality.

Love on a Brick: with thanks to Vaughan Fisher for the brick.

Are We There Yet? was commissioned by the Red Room Company for its series The Poet's Life Works' (2009) and was performed and reproduced as part of that project under the title "But the Poet's Life Would Work Better If…"

Rainforest Triptych was written for the "Poets and Painters" exhibition and reading, at the Bett Gallery, Hobart, August 2013. It accompanied the painting "The Black at the Heart of the Sassafras" by Tim Burns.

Fall, Prince Edward Island: Anne (line 7) is she of Green Gables, not at all "demure, to be walked on."

Principles: Kath Fallon's character was in the excellent novel *Paydirt* (UWA Press, 2007). Racine, "Point d'argent, point de Suisse" in Les Plaideurs (1668), his only comedy. The title of Redgum's first album, *If You Don't Fight You Lose*, was taken from a line in their song "Killing Floor". Mest is a Chicago based punk/rock band.

Scratched in Stone is part of the anthology and exhibition *One Hundred Years Since Gallipoli*, collected and curated by Graeme Lindsay.

Piraeus: This is the third poem of a series. The others are "Red Label" (I Con, Salt Publishing, 2008, p196) and "Write the Future" (Yeah No, PressPress, 2012, p15). The murder of Alexandros Grigoropoulos, aged 15, by a police officer was the immediate cause of the Greek riots in 2008.

Revenge: Steve Irwin was killed by a stingray in 2006. A few days later Peter Brock, Australian racing car driver, died when his Holden car ran into a tree at high speed.

"The Unspeak Poems" owes its title and inspiration to Steven Poole, *Unspeak*™, (Little, Brown, London, 2006).

Nature Poem: Stelarc is an Australian performance artist, some of whose work consists of modifications to his own body.

Anthrax Street, Lafayette TN: Cipro (ciprofloxacin) is an antibacterial medication.

Fair and Balanced: United Airlines Flight 93 was to have been the third aircraft used in the attacks on the USA on 11 September 2001.

Taking Queen Victoria to Inveresk: These three poems are based on paintings from the collection of the Queen Victoria Museum and Art Gallery, Launceston: *Fruit and Flowers*, William Buelow Gould (1850), *Sunday in the Gardens*, Ethel Carrick Fox (1907) *and Naming the Sensation* No. 2, Angela Brennan (1995).

Naming the Sensation No. 2: "JP" is Jackson Pollock.

Autumn: Valvins was where Mallarmé died.

Five Trees: The "Tasman Limited" was a Tasmanian passenger express train.

The Worst Journey in the World: See Apsley Cherry-Garrard's book of the same title for a fuller account of this strange expedition.

Vanzetti: It was Judge Thayer who sentenced Sacco and Vanzetti to death for a crime which they patently did not commit.

Whatever Happened to Conway Twitty?: "Stan the Man" was Stan Rofe, one of Australia's first rock 'n' roll radio DJs.

Man and Law: The quotation in stanza 2 is of the opening couplet of Verlaine's "O Triste, Triste Etait Mon Ame" from *Romances Sans Paroles*.

The Atlas:
III: "The mountain" is Mt Direction, as viewed from Montrose across the Derwent. Hoess was camp commander at Auschwitz for a time, formerly at Dachau and before that a prisoner himself,

having been convicted of murder.

Interlude: Greystone is the hospital in New York where Woody Guthrie was visited by Bob Dylan in 1961. The second stanza of this interlude is for the voice of Guthrie, the third for that of Dylan.

XVI: The Mannlicher-Carcano 91/38 was the weapon alleged to have been in Lee Harvey Oswald's possession on the day of John Kennedy's assassination.

Songs of the Protest Era: Song My is the name of the cluster of villages which included My Lai, which was destroyed by American marines in March 1968 when over 300 unarmed civilians, mostly children, were massacred.

Song for Seychelles: "The last bearded corsair" was Sir James Mancham, the first President of Seychelles, who spent most of his term of office in luxury in the South of France until deposed by a coup in 1977.

A Letter to Egon Kisch: Egon Kisch, a Czech national and a Jew, had been deported from Nazi Germany in 1933. He travelled the world, speaking and writing on important political issues, coming to Australia in 1934 at the invitation of the Movement Against War and Fascism. The Australian Government, through Attorney-General Robert Menzies and Immigration Minister Eric Harrison, refused him entry. Kisch jumped off his ship to the Port Melbourne wharf, breaking his leg in the process, and challenged the ban in the courts. He won and spent four months here. His book, *Australian Landfall*, published in 1937, remains one of the most perceptive and entertaining accounts of this country. After living in Mexico for several years, Egon Kisch died in Czechoslovakia in 1948.

Gnomic: Garden gnomes in the likeness of former AFL footballer Ben Cousins without the tattoo are more common, but bring less on eBay.

Elegy for Shelton: Shelton Lea, poet (1946-2005)

Little Patagonia: Faustroll and Panmuphle are characters in Alfred Jarry's novel *Exploits and Opinions of Dr Faustroll, Pataphysician*. 'Pushing a Good Thing Too Far' and 'Dance, Puppet, Dance' were hit songs by Little Pattie.

Little Patefaction: Patefaction is the act or state of opening up or disclosure.

Little Patchouli: 'The science of imaginary solutions' is a definition of pataphysics suggested by Jarry.

Little Patible: The patible is the shorter, transverse arm of a traditional Christian cross.

Little Patrician: Chrissy Amphlett, Little Pattie's first cousin, was lead singer of the Divinyls.

Little Patrick White: Stanza 3: see Patrick White, *Riders in the Chariot*, p269.

Little Patmos: Lines 5 & 6, see 'The Revelation of St John the Divine', 13:1.

Tim & Stephanie, 1968

www.ingramcontent.com/pod-product-compliance
Lightning Source LLC
Chambersburg PA
CBHW020755160426
43192CB00006B/333